Chewy

The Street Dog Who Brought
a Neighbourhood Together

BRUCE KLEIN

EBURY
PRESS

1 3 5 7 9 10 8 6 4 2

First published in 2014 by Ebury Press, an imprint of Ebury Publishing
A Random House Group company

Copyright © Bruce and Lauren Klein 2014

Bruce and Lauren Klein have asserted their right to be identified as the authors of
this Work in accordance with the Copyright, Designs and Patents Act 1988

The Random House Group Limited Reg. No. 954009

Addresses for companies within the Random House Group can be found at
www.randomhouse.co.uk

A CIP catalogue record for this book is available from the British Library

Th. . . . . Stewardship
Council . . . . isation. Our
books ca . . . . C is the only
forest-ce . . . . rganisations,
including Greenpeace. Our . . . procurement policy can be found at
www.randomhouse.co.uk/environment

Printed and bound by CPI Group (UK) Ltd, Croydon, CR0 4YY

ISBN 9780091957056

To buy books by your favourite authors and register for offers visit
www.randomhouse.co.uk

This book is dedicated to

Cecelia French

Chewy's Guardian Angel

Contents

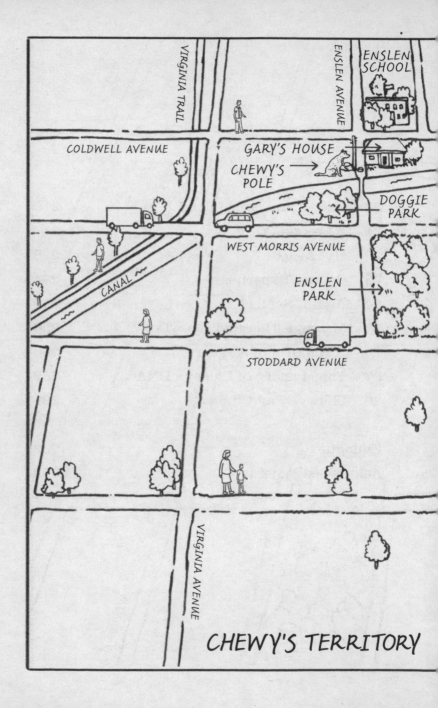

VIRGINIA TRAIL

ENSLEN AVENUE

ENSLEN SCHOOL

COLDWELL AVENUE

GARY'S HOUSE

CHEWY'S POLE

DOGGIE PARK

WEST MORRIS AVENUE

CANAL

ENSLEN PARK

STODDARD AVENUE

VIRGINIA AVENUE

CHEWY'S TERRITORY

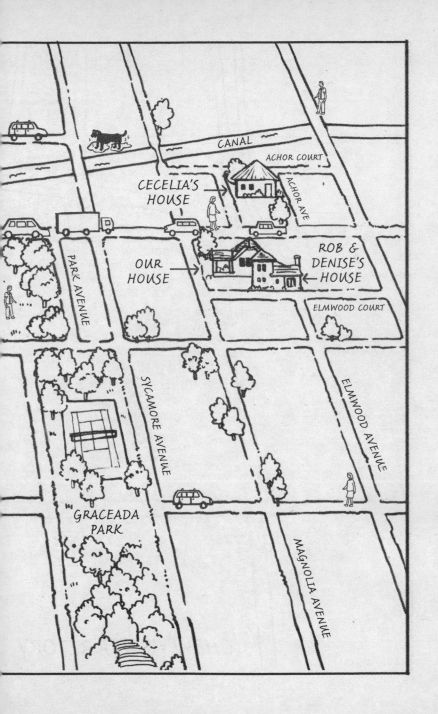

CANAL

ACHOR COURT

ACHOR AVE

CECELIA'S HOUSE

ROB & DENISE'S HOUSE

OUR HOUSE

PARK AVENUE

ELMWOOD COURT

ELMWOOD AVENUE

SYCAMORE AVENUE

GRACEADA PARK

MAGNOLIA AVENUE

Chapter One

Love at First Sight

'Look at that beautiful dog!' I said to my wife.

His reddish brown mane sparkled, then he disappeared. I looked out the car window, searching for him. He was gone in the shadows, hidden in the walking legs behind the chairs set out for sale, then behind the US postal mail box. Suddenly his head and shoulders stepped out into sunlight, his big chest held high. He stopped at the corner like any pedestrian and stood looking around excitedly, his tongue lolling, relaxed.

We were late for our matinee movie. Lauren was driving and it was a beautiful California July day. The light at McHenry Avenue and J Street changed suddenly, forcing us to stop. 'Perfect,' my wife said, shifting into low.

But I was looking out the window at Chewy, mesmerised.

Ten, nine, eight, seven... I strummed my fingers on the dashboard.

The pedestrian walk sign flashed down to zero. Then the tweet, tweet, tweet sound for the deaf bleeped. Two young women in tight skirts stepped up behind Chewy.

They didn't notice how they spooked him. He stepped back, away from the corner into the shadow of the restaurant behind him.

'Whose dog is that?' I wondered, rolling the window down. I couldn't believe anyone would let a beautiful dog like that wander loose.

'Where?' Lauren asked (my body blocked her view). 'I don't see him,' she added.

'Over there,' I said, pointing my arm to the corner across the street just as the light changed.

'What are you talking about?' my wife said, annoyed.

I leaned back against the seat for her to see.

'Oh, that helps a lot,' she said, turning. 'I don't see anything.'

Of course she didn't. We'd lunged through the intersection by the time she looked.

'You missed him. He was sooo beautiful!'

'Are you kidding me?' she said, shifting into second.

'Go back,' I said, 'you'll see.'

I turned to look out the window to see if he was still there.

'Not on your life,' my wife said, 'we'll be late!'

* * *

The movie was a dud, its images boring, its dialogue flat, but Chewy's image was alive in my head. It haunted me every time I drove downtown. Going to the bank, I'd drive out of my way to the corner where I first saw him, hoping he'd be there. Visiting a local shop to buy an egg timer, I'd swing by Chewy's corner, looking for him. No luck. Each time I returned a library book, I'd scan the streets hoping to see him. Not that I became obsessed with him, just interested. I couldn't get his image out of my mind. Who would own such a beautiful dog and let him wander the streets?

Sooner or later he'd get hit by a car or put down by the pound. I thought about scavenging the pound but that was too weird. Besides we already had one dog, Emma.

So I let it go.

Actually, I'd been preoccupied. The year before my prostate specific antigen suddenly increased rapidly, a telltale marker for aggressive prostate cancer. After a brief period of watchful waiting, the doctors removed my prostate the following January. The cancer seemed encapsulated; my five-year survival rate high.

After the operation I started taking evening walks to regain my health. And it was on one of these, several months later, at the end of summer that Chewy magically reappeared. I was looping home over the bridge by the canal. As I walked up the cul de sac towards the bridge an elderly couple walked past me.

'That your dog?' the man asked.

'What dog?'

'That dog – he's been following us.'

I looked round to where he was pointing. There was just enough light to see. In the middle of the street, about twenty feet from us, was the beautiful chestnut dog. Light and shadows flickered across his body as dusk settled in. Hearing our voices he turned around and trotted back to stand by the telegraph pole near the bridge. Even in diminished light he was beautiful.

Oh, my God, I said to myself.

'He seems gentle enough but you never know,' the woman said. She walked with two of those steel-tipped ski poles to steady herself. Her hair was pulled back into a bun, her jawline tight. No rooster's goblet hanging under her throat, unlike mine.

'He's probably gentle,' she added. 'He followed us halfway home last night.'

'Oh, really?' I absentmindedly tightened my jawline.

'Well,' the husband said, looking at me, 'nice meeting you.' He held out his hand. We shook. Then he steadied his wife's elbow and turned down the cul de sac towards Enslen School. I watched them go for a second, then turned towards Chewy, thinking how excited my wife would be to meet this dog.

He eyed me from a distance, wary but interested.

In the late evening light he was so handsome: his red-brown fur glowed, his white muzzle, speckled with freckles, gave him an engaging look. Standing tall, his four paws dipped white, the creamy white tip of his tail waved like a metronome, a final splash of white swirled across his shoulders and down his chest crest. He came up to greet me.

4

'Oh, you're beautiful,' I said in soothing tones. 'Who would let you wander the streets alone?' But he didn't move and instead looked at me quizzically like he knew me or wanted to. He lifted his head up and leaned slightly forwards, eyes scrutinising me, wet black nostrils sniffing the air for my human smell.

I knew my scents would tell him everything he needed to know. What that was, I had no idea. My brain was in overdrive. Was he searching for the smells of his former master? Or had his first owners simply opened their car door and dumped him on the street, abandoning him as a puppy? Had he run away, following some scent? Was he just hungry when he sniffed me? Maybe he was not looking for a home or a human family. Might he be sniffing the scents of our dog, Emma, or for his dog family – his mother, his father? Was he just another dog who had wandered away in exuberant playfulness and been orphaned to the streets? I just shook my head at how unfathomable it all was.

He seemed so friendly, so gentle. As I walked closer to pet him, he moved quickly backwards. He moved quickly backwards again, then stopped.

'I'm not going to hurt you,' I said. My gentle tone must have intrigued him. He stood contemplating me. His eyes darted up at me and then down, as if he was saying, 'Who are you? Can I trust you?' They fixed on me just for a moment longer, and then he turned away. In that moment I saw in his eyes a painful sadness, a flickering desire for human contact, for warmth, perhaps companionship, and a naked vulnerability that deeply touched me. And then it was gone. His eyes darkened – all the sadness of the world seemed to be there.

Then I caught myself. I told myself rationally that I was projecting my feelings onto him. Something else inside me was moved, though; something had changed.

Then he wandered off down the canal.

He's a mystery dog, Lauren needs to see this dog, I thought to myself.

* * *

When I got home I immediately found Lauren.

'I saw that beautiful dog.'

'Really?' Lauren asked, her interest piqued. 'What dog?'

'The dog we saw downtown.'

Lauren looked at me like I was a bit touched. 'What dog that we saw downtown? I don't remember any of this.'

'Well, you never saw him.'

'Uh, huh,' came her sceptical response.

'It doesn't matter, I just saw him again. You will love him – he is just your kind of dog.'

Chapter Two
Chewy's Patch

Three days later circling the same way home, I met Gary and his neighbour, Michele. Gary stood watering his lawn. He lived in the corner house opposite the electrical sub-station and next to the canal and bridge. Chewy, as they told me he was called, was standing in the middle of Enslen Avenue, which butted up against the canal in between the station and Gary's house. Gary had been feeding Chewy, and he told me that his dog Ginger had befriended him. The three of us, Michele, Gary and me, were all looking at Chewy. He looked like a Saint Bernard/Border Collie mix.

'He's so beautiful,' Michele said.

I agree, I thought to myself.

I reached out to pet him. Chewy turned away, walking towards his telegraph pole.

'Be careful, don't spook him,' warned Gary. He clicked his mouth and held out his hand.

Chewy came up to him, Gary twisted a knot in his hose and threw the hose down to scratch Chewy's head. Chewy ducked Gary's hand and stepped back.

'He's still a little jittery,' Gary said, 'but people feed him. I feed him. Hell, the whole neighbourhood feeds him!' He smiled.

Suddenly I noticed everything: blankets, water bowls and random piles of dog food littered the sidewalk in front of the electrical substation. Nearer Gary's house, on his verge, there were three striped blankets beside a small pile of kibble; also a partially deflated soccer ball that had burst open and was kicked into Gary's bushes.

Ginger, Gary's dog, came waddling up. Black, over-weight, muzzle fringed with grey, she had smelt food.

I heard two couples rambling over the bridge. When they saw us looking at them, the first man said, 'Hello, you feeding him too?' He smiled as he walked by.

'He smells these bone marrow bits,' Gary said. He held out his hand to show me the three penny-sized bone marrow bits that lay in his hand. Gary's hands were beefy, his fingers thick. I'd seen hands like that when I'd worked in the steel mills in Gary, Indiana. Labourer hands. Gary saw me staring at them.

'Yeah, I used to box,' he said.

'That sport,' I responded, 'can chew your face up.'

'You wanna see chewed up? Leave your slippers out overnight.' He pointed at Chewy. 'I did and guess who chewed them up?'

Chewy raised his head higher, sniffing Gary's hand.

'Oh!' I said. 'I'd guessed Chewy's name was from Chewbacca in *Star Wars*.'

'You guessed wrong! Chewy is for my little friend here who chewed up my slippers.'

Gary lowered his hand full of bone marrow treats. The ads for these treats say lip-smacking good but with Chewy it was more like head-tilting-and-nostril-flaring good. He delicately lifted a bone marrow treat from Gary's hand and stepped back. His teeth crushed the bone marrow until it fell to bits on the asphalt. Then he ate them at his leisure. One by one, he slowly gobbled up the smaller bits, savouring the taste. Definitely a dog with style and a certain class.

He must be starving, I thought. *Look at his legs. Maybe he has hip dysplasia.*

Chewy stopped eating. He came forward to Gary's outstretched fingers and sniffed at the second and third treat they held before exquisitely lifting both from his hand.

* * *

Well-to-do professionals and blue-collar workers live in our neighbourhood. Families with kids, young married couples without, empty nesters whose kids have left, single people, young and old, grandmas and grandpas live here.

Lauren and I live a few blocks from both Graceada and Enslen parks. She loves this neighbourhood. Graceada Park has a concert bowl at one end used for popular 'Concert in the Park' events during the summer.

In summertime children's movies are shown there when it starts getting dark. There's a large picnic pavilion for family and civic events. Celebrations like Fourth of July, Earth Day and Diversity Days are held in the park. The two parks are heavily used on weekends for family picnics.

On weekdays a lovely grammar school, Enslen, is active with children attending classes, from the ages of five to eleven years old. Built in 1929, it has been lovingly maintained and is still fully functional today. In fact, it is one of the better grammar schools in town.

The younger couples flocked to Modesto during the 2000 housing boom, remodelling smaller houses, adding extra rooms, grandmother cottages or second storeys. The neighbourhood is unique in that the majority of the homes retain their original style: Arts and Crafts, early American Colonial and old Spanish-style houses. Trees are decades old, front lawns and gardens expressing their owners' style.

Lauren was born in Modesto and worked as a Certified Public Accountant. I'm a painter, a fine artist, born in Indiana, and I taught in Alameda. We met in San Francisco at the gallery where Lauren used to work and which handled my *en plein air* landscapes. I liked her spunk. After marrying, Lauren took night-school courses for several years to earn her CPA licence. High living costs in the San Francisco Bay area forced us in 2002 to move to Modesto. We bought Lauren's auntie's old house, which we've been rehabbing ever since. After ten years of serious rehabbing, our house still needed new floors, a new kitchen and a long list of improvements that Lauren kept updating.

A few years ago the old railroad tracks that ran on the northwest side of our neighbourhood on a street called Virginia Avenue were removed. A walking and bike trail took their place. This new trail enhanced the area. People walk, run, exercise and most importantly, walk their dogs on it. It seems like half the households in our neighbourhood have either a dog or cat. Greeting fellow dog walkers, you learn their dogs' names and sometimes the owner's name. These casual meetings lead to friendships and a loose network of dog lovers. We believe Chewy's first home was along this walking and bike trail. Several neighbours saw him hiding in the oleander bushes along the railroad track before the trail was built.

Modesto sits in the San Joaquin Valley, or the southern portion of the Central Valley. Twenty-five miles to the west is the Diablo range of mountains, and many do the daily 180-mile round trip commute over them to the San Francisco Bay area beyond. I do it twice a week, driving to Alameda where I still teach. Fifty miles to the east of Modesto is the High Sierra Mountains, containing amazing landmarks such as Yosemite National Park, where Lauren and I married. Melted snow from the Sierras creates highly fertile agricultural land in the San Joaquin valley.

Fresh fruits – apples, oranges, grapes, almonds, apricots – and all sorts of vegetables are grown on local ranches and farms. These join baked delicacies – artisanbreads, ethnic foods from local bakeries and restaurants – in Modesto's downtown farmer's market. Usually a guitarist and vocalist perform live during the market. Other vendors sell their baskets or plants.

Summers are hot in the San Joaquin Valley, in the 30s and upwards to 40 degrees Celsius. People stay indoors, turning on air conditioning during the day. Evenings with light breezes are lovely for walking or bike riding in shorts and tank tops. People sit outside on the front porch, relax and watch the neighbourhood. Evenings or weekends, they barbecue in their backyards. Ice cream vendors in their vans or on bikes ride the neighbourhood, dinging bells. Children rush up to buy ice cream in the warm night air. Come fall and winter, residents bundle up against the fog, rain or wind.

Sounds too clichéd, or too nostalgic? There are treelined streets and deep small-town middle-class values in our community. They evoke stereotypical images and peaceful living but the truth is Modesto is much more complicated. The community is also beset with serious problems. Our air quality is poor – smog from the greater San Francisco Bay Area blows inland and settles over Modesto, adding to the poor air quality, at times making it unhealthy for residents by causing breathing difficulties and aggravating allergies. Politically, the Central Valley has never been able to compete with Southern California or the San Francisco Bay Area for wealth, jobs or political influence. So, Southern California and San Francisco Bay concerns normally trump ours in terms of government statewide issues. We make do with less. With steep budget cuts, our poor and struggling residents find their safety nets shredded. Our unemployment rate is higher than the state and national averages; our high-school dropout rate is also higher. Additionally, crime is a major concern for many residents: as many as 5,000 gang members live in Stanislaus County, in and around Modesto.

But the residents in our neighbourhood do tackle these serious issues, individually and in civic organisations. For example, to fight crime some of the neighbourhoods have formed crime-watch committees and hired a private security company to supplement police patrols. When apartment buildings threatened the architectural character, neighbours got together to stop them being built.

On a whole host of issues, from cleaning up trash through providing free dental care to providing food for the homeless, the good citizens of Modesto, individually and in volunteer organisations like Rotary and Habitat for Humanity, work hard to stabilise and keep alive the small town middle-class family-oriented values that Modesto represents. In short, these healthy responses keep alive one vein of the American Dream in a complex stew of conflicting trends.

In some ways then it shouldn't have been unexpected that a significant section of our neighbours spontaneously acted to feed, protect and help rescue Chewy.

Chapter Three

Cecelia, Animal Lover Extraordinaire

The real hero in this story is Cecelia. Cecelia French is a sweet, warm and generous person. She fed Chewy daily before we ever did. Her mission was always to save him.

'Dogs are special,' she said when I first met her. 'Chewy is above that. Of course, he is beautiful, extra-special beautiful, but he has something else…' Her eyes shifted downwards as she paused, thinking for a moment. 'If you watch him playing with other dogs you would know what I mean: he's so joyous, so happy playing. He's not just like other dogs but somehow more than just that, more like an angel. I don't know what words to use… You just have to see him.'

I knew what she meant. I'd seen him playing. It wasn't just his puppy exuberance or his physical beauty, it was the way Chewy played with other dogs. His play was gentle, confident and sharing. When you watched him you wished your own life had more of that quality.

I have watched plenty of other dogs play. Chewy's play wasn't one dog trying to dominate the other. Play for Chewy went like this: after their initial greeting, Chewy would display a common dog behaviour called 'Play Bow'. In her book *What Dogs Want*, Arden Moore describes this behaviour as a happy dog plopping down with his front legs extended and his rear end pushed up in the air – a 'let's play' sign for dogs. Chewy would jump forward a bit, barking, and then when the other dog gave chase he'd quickly wiggle away into a run, usually at an angle so he could watch the other dogs approach. Or quite often, he'd take off in a long run, circling and weaving in and out of trees, barking and gaining speed if the other dog caught up. It was as if he enjoyed the other dog on its own terms, whatever they might be. Too aggressive dogs or dogs trying to dominate spoiled the fun. He would set them straight with a low growl. 'Play fair or there's no play at all,' he seemed to say; a Chewy doggie rule. Other dogs wised up or simply walked away. Chewy also has a knack of avoiding confrontation. Gary had noticed this: 'He avoids trouble. If there is trouble brewing, Chewy goes the other way.'

Cecelia lives four blocks from us. We didn't know her before Chewy entered our lives, but Cecelia and Lauren think alike about animals. They both rescue strays, which means they have too many animals and spend too much money on them. I'm sure Lauren and I must have seen Cecelia walking in the neighbourhood, we must have smiled or waved to one another as we passed each other by. Both Cecelia and Lauren were dog people, each of them religiously walked their dogs – how could their paths not have crossed before? One reason is they walked different paths around the neighbourhood. Cecelia favoured the canal bank, while Lauren chose the neighbourhood streets, partially so she could see how the neighbours were fixing up their old houses.

At the time Cecelia was trying to help Chewy she was sixty-five years old and close to retirement. She and her sister, Charlotte, were living together with various cats and dogs. Cecelia is a small person. Her heritage is Portuguese and she has curly dark hair that is greying with age and a lovely open face. Being a mother, a grandmother, a nurse and an animal rescuer, it's not hard to see the nurturing side of her – it resonates in her mannerisms and speech. She also has her feet firmly placed on the ground and is practical. Being a single mother and a nurse has exposed her to the realities of this world. Single-handedly she proudly raised her daughter, putting her through school and giving her the opportunity to become successful in life as a corporate attorney. Cecelia has a quiet strength.

Cecelia first saw Chewy sitting under a palm tree on the canal bank. She was walking Max, her black and white Lhasa Apso mix, up the sidewalk to the canal after work. Suddenly, Max growled, and lunged. His leash pulled him up short. He stood up on his hind legs, paws flaying in the air, his growl deepening.

'Oh, Maxie, stop it, just stop it!' Cecelia said as she looked up. She pulled hard on Max's leash.

Chewy stood up, glanced at them and took off, running down the canal.

'Maxie,' Cecelia said, tightening her grip on his leash, 'Stop it. You're a very rude dog, a very rude dog. He's much bigger than you.' She watched Chewy run. He paused to look over his shoulder for a second, then lunged forwards, running down the canal.

I wonder what his story is? I hope he is all right, she thought.

Two weeks later, when Cecelia saw Chewy again while walking Max, she stopped on the canal bridge to watch Chewy greet people. Then she crossed the bridge and sat down on the kerb opposite, thinking how she might rescue him. *Oh*, she thought, *I can feed him each morning, or each day after work. And if no one else rescues him, I will – Max and the other two dogs will just have to adjust*, 'Won't you, Maxie. You'll just have to make room for him.' Max sat at her feet. 'That would be no small feat, Maxie, no small feat at all – you with your bossy little-dog complex attitude.'

She reached down to pet her dog.

* * *

That night Cecelia started cooking. Max immediately knew something was afoot. Suddenly tantalising aromas pervaded the kitchen: fresh olive oil, sautéing chicken breasts, cottage cheese mixed with cornflakes and freshly crumbled breadcrumbs. Cecelia came from the kitchen with a plate in her hands, bent over and gave him a little treat. *Right here at my feet. Oh boy, oh boy, what could be better?* Max thought, wagging his tail.

Each night after work Cecelia cooked Chewy chicken breasts. Her fingers pulled the meat off its bone, cutting up the breasts, sautéing them and then of course sampling a piece. When they were done she put all the chicken pieces in a plastic container, and mixed the other ingredients in before snapping the lid shut. *That's what they have in dog food. Chewy will like this*, she thought. In the morning she'd drive over to feed Chewy before she went to work. This had been her routine for three weeks before we met her.

Chewy would lie waiting. He'd wrap his body around the telegraph pole and watch for her. At night he'd sleep in the dirt near the bushes along Gary's fence. He had burrowed a shallow indentation in the earth. Burrowing kept his underside warm by the earth and dry.

It's hard to tell who enjoyed the visits more, Chewy or Cecelia herself. But one experience made it clear. One morning, taking water for herself and packing Chewy's food in a grocery bag, Cecelia set off down the five blocks to Chewy's patch from her house. This Saturday morning, the slight breeze coming in her car window was cool. It was fall. By October, the intense Central Valley summer heat was over for another year. The street was deserted. Driving down Coldwell Avenue, the sun raked the tree-tops. As she drove, Cecelia wondered how Chewy was.

Meanwhile, Chewy lay fast asleep on the grass in the front yard of Enslen School. He knew nothing of Cecelia coming until he smelled chicken. *Food*, he thought. His head rose, sniffing the cool morning air. *Yes, yes*, his nostrils flared, *food*. His eyes opened alertly as he lifted his head, scanning the air again. There she was, Cecelia.

When her car came near, he pranced up alongside, looking at her through the open window as she drove. Chewy's head was up and sniffing. His big brown eye sparkled with energy, soft and wide, staring, as it bounced up and down outside alongside Cecelia's window.

Driving quietly, Cecelia thought how nice it would be to see Chewy again and know he'd made it through another night on the streets. Suddenly she had the uncanny feeling of being watched. Out of the corner of her eye she looked to the left in her side mirror: nothing. She glanced in her rear view mirror: nothing. Then a flicker of a black nose caught her attention and she heard a familiar bark. When she glanced to her right she saw a large furry brown head, bobbing up and down alongside her car.

'Chewy!' she exclaimed.

Chewy's big brown eye was staring at her. Then his eye disappeared, reappeared, disappeared again. Chewy was trotting alongside her car. The eye came up, seemed to hang in the air, as if time had been suspended. It looked at her again and then dropped out of sight. Confused, Cecelia gasped.

'Oh, my God!' she screamed at her car window.

'Chewy, Chewy my angel, Chewy!' Cecilia exclaimed, stunned.

She couldn't believe her eyes. Chewy was running alongside her car. *He must have seen me driving and smelt the food*, she thought. She noticed he had come from the direction of the school near the front grass. *What a dear, he ran out to greet me.*

Her car swerved over the midline of the street. Cecelia grabbed the steering wheel tighter and straightened the car. Thankfully there was no accident. She tried to calm herself. When she looked out again Chewy's furry head was still bobbing up and down alongside her car. She was not driving fast; she thought about pulling over or stopping but since she could not see all of him she thought she might make matters worse and hit him accidentally. Better to keep going slowly.

Chewy continued to run along the side of Cecelia's car in the middle of the street, trotting down Coldwell Ave. Instinctively, Cecelia pulled to the left to avoid hitting him. Luckily the street was empty; there were no parked cars or oncoming cars approaching. In tandem then, Cecelia driving slowly, checking for Chewy's bobbing head and eye; Chewy trotting beside her car, checking for Cecelia's face and food scents.

Nervously moving forwards, Cecelia's fingers continued to grip the steering wheel hard, bracing her arms, holding the car's line straight. Looking in her rear view mirror she saw there was no traffic behind her. *Slow down, slow down*, she told herself. *Drive straight and don't swerve*. She kept her eyes on the road with no car coming in the opposite direction. What if a big truck comes? Chewy could be killed. Cecelia could just see the accident. She gripped the steering wheel tight, her knuckles turning white. Her body leaned over the steering wheel. It was a clear morning. Just one more turn to go...

At the corner of Enslen and Coldwell she turned left in a slow, small and tight arch to give Chewy the largest possible area to turn in. *Is he still there?* she anxiously wondered.

She looked for him out the side window. *Where, where has he gone? Oh my God, I've run over him*! Cecelia spun her head left and right. He'd disappeared.

Chewy had cut behind Cecelia's car and run along safely on the sidewalk. Now, he stood in the street smiling as she parked.

When Cecelia jumped out of her car, elated, she wanted to run up and hug him. 'Oh, you're a good boy Chewy, such a good boy,' she said instead.

Chewy could not be hugged yet. He was still trying to figure out these humans, whether they were trustworthy or not. Cecelia settled for putting out his food and water bowls and then watched him.

One bit of joy, one moment of terror.

* * *

Ginger, Gary's dog, and Chewy developed a friendship. Who knows how or why? Strays typically are loners. Did Chewy choose Gary's house near the canal bridge as a home because of Ginger? Possibly. Perhaps Ginger gave companionship, or it was Gary giving Ginger food, which Chewy could eat? Ginger most certainly had a part in it. She lived in the front yard; she was always there for Chewy.

Why did Chewy choose this spot as his? Perhaps the foot traffic across the bridge in the early morning and late afternoon afforded him the possible option of finding a human home. Since there was only a foot-bridge over the canal on Enslen Avenue the road stopped at the canal. Chewy choose a spot where there were fewer cars, it was safe.

'That dog felt that it was his home turf – he had that sense of home,' Mike, our veterinarian, explained to us as we talked to him about Chewy one day. 'If dogs are familiar with the area, they will stay in the area. If they are not familiar with the area, they will keep on going.'

But Chewy stayed. Close to Ginger's companionship, and close to Cecelia.

Cecelia always brought extra food for Ginger. Ginger was older, overweight and slower. If Cecelia just left Chewy's home-cooked chicken and food on the kerb, Ginger would wander over and begin to eat the food. So, instead Cecelia brought Ginger milk bones as her special treat... A few of these hand-fed treats satisfied Ginger.

Chewy often watched the whole scenario before he came over to eat. It was as if he had good manners; he let his host eat first. Graciously, he would eat after Ginger. A ritual developed.

Initially, Cecelia placed Chewy's bowl stuffed with treats ten feet away when feeding him. Over time she slowly moved the bowl closer to her until finally the bowl and Chewy were next to her. Chewy was within stroking range while he ate. Slowly, Chewy allowed Cecelia to stroke him; first behind the shoulders, then along his muzzle and finally, light strokes on his head. Not always and not for long periods. Cecelia never assumed Chewy would allow her to stroke him. Each day stroking had to be negotiated; petting him on his side was not allowed.

Cecelia would often feed Chewy by holding her palm up and placing a piece of chicken in it for Chewy to retrieve. She would continue to talk to Chewy, letting him know what a beautiful and good dog he was. Chewy came up tentatively, sniffed the chicken and licked it. Then very delicately, like a skilled surgeon, he turned his head sideways ever so lightly. His front teeth were just touching the chicken breast. He rolled his tongue out just beyond the piece, flipping it so that it pushed the chicken breast against his big incisors and lifting the morsel off Cecelia's hand gently, so delicately, so silently it was as if he were lifting a feather from her hand. You would swear his gentle touch was so as not to bruise, bite or even scratch Cecelia's hand. It was as if he'd taken a fragile Fabergé egg from her palm. He would then glance up at Cecelia and back away with his chicken morsel.

Chewy, you are the gentlest dog I know, Cecelia would think to herself. Then she'd put her hand down at her side and watch Chewy eat. *How strange to be sitting on a deserted street on a Saturday morning feeding this beautiful stray dog. My life is a bit strange, but wonderful!*

'What a gift you have given me, Chewy,' she said. 'Thank you, thank you.'

Chapter Four
A Strange Man

One late afternoon a week later, while feeding Chewy, a strange man walked towards Cecelia. *Look at him*, she thought. *Who wears jeans splattered with paint?* The jeans were old, torn at the knees and they were dirty. His sweatshirt in no better shape. *Is he homeless?* she wondered. *What's he up to?* She was sitting on the kerb with Chewy. Chewy saw this man and backed away. Cecelia mentally prepared herself for flight. When this strange-looking man suddenly changed his course, walking diagonally towards her, she thought, *I'd better get up and leave. Yes, I'd better be on my way!*

She gathered up the chicken bits and food, put them in the plastic container, snapped the lid on tight, checking with her fingers that it was tight all the way around. She didn't want any accidents. Then she stood up quickly.

'Is that your dog?' the strange man asked. Before she could leave he stepped right in front of her. He appeared to be in his sixties, six feet tall, thin and balding. He wore glasses. Cecelia did not like the look of him.

'Is that your dog?' he persisted, a little more insistently.

But his voice was gentle and his stress soft. *Maybe I don't have anything to worry about*, Cecilia thought. *He seems OK after all.* She looked at him for a moment. *Was that my dog?* she repeated to herself. *No, not yet. Perhaps Chewy will be my dog soon.*

'No, this dog is a stray,' she said. 'I'm feeding him. He belongs to no one. I'm trying to get him off the streets.'

It was getting late. Time to head home.

Across the canal, a skinny adolescent boy with no shirt and a moussed-up haircut did wheelies across the canal bridge and down the canal embankment past them. They both watched wide-eyed. The kid smirked, riding by.

'You've been feeding him?' the stranger asked. He introduced himself. 'I'm Bruce.'

'Yes, I've been feeding him,' Cecelia said, relaxing.

Cecilia and Bruce talked for another half an hour, sharing experiences about Chewy before exchanging telephone numbers and addresses.

Bruce wanted Lauren to meet Cecelia. She was an interesting woman, a dog lover like his wife. She'd gone to so much trouble to get to know Chewy. She was someone Lauren would like. When Bruce got home that evening he was excited.

* * *

I stood in the bedroom doorway as Lauren sat up in bed, still sick with bronchitis. Her cats were glued to her body, purring. Looking at them, I thought, *It's true animals can sense when you're sick.* I looked at the cats, wondering, *Are they doing hourly shifts, twenty-four hours a day?* Fred was on her legs, then Fred got up to go take a break and Gracie moved over to sit on her lap. Rudy's turn was later, the night shift.

I imagined hearing them. 'Boy,' Fred says, 'am I beat!' He stretches full length and climbs down the covers. 'Sleeping all day is tough. But hey, this ain't the cat's meow, it's hard work. Gracie, it's your shift. Watch her breathing – she'll turn on you suddenly if you don't watch out. We got to love her healthy. Remember, she's our meal ticket. Without her, we're out in the street.' 'I got it covered,' Gracie says, 'Great job, Fred, she looks happy. You made my shift easier.'

I smiled to myself. Lauren looked up at me.

'They both died in the end,' she said.

'What?' I answered, confused.

'You know, I figured this one out five pages before the end. All the clues, the little seemingly insignificant details fell into place. The suspense was killing me so I had to figure it out.'

'Oh, really?'

'Yes, and I was right. I'm usually not. But this mystery puzzle I figured out. I love the suspense and solving the mystery,' she said.

I noticed she hadn't coughed once. Her chills were apparently gone; a week in bed and she was ready to go back to work. Got to give those cats their due. A purring love potion is better than any antibiotic.

'Oh, you know me,' Lauren said. 'Just give me suspense and a complicated mystery and I'm happy. I can escape from the real world for a while. Sometimes getting sick isn't half bad.'

Yep, her chills were gone, her coughing less frequent. And she was feisty as ever.

'Look, I met this woman while I was out walking,' I said. 'She's nice. She loves animals as much as you do.' Lauren looked at me quizzically. 'Plus, you remember me talking about that beautiful dog? I saw him again, he's a really neat dog.'

Lauren perked up. I guess for me to mention another dog, and a dog that I was excited about, meant there might be a possibility of getting another dog. Emma, our first dog, was getting older. Lauren had been trying to convince me that another dog might help keep Emma young.

'You should see him, he might still be there. Do you want to drive over and see this dog?'

'Give me a second,' Lauren said. 'I'll get dressed and be in my car before you've locked the front door.'

Lauren dressed before I could change my mind. *A dog for Emma, a beautiful dog. What has come over Bruce? I love him, but he's a strange man. Who knows what he's thinking? Life is certainly not boring being married to Bruce!* Lauren smiled to herself.

Whatever had come over me, Lauren was excited. She was waiting in the car when I locked the front door. 'See,' she said, 'I told you.'

* * *

We drove in Lauren's car over the bridge and down Coldwell Avenue until the houses ended at the canal on Enslen Avenue. Lauren parked and opened her car door.

'I don't see him,' she exclaimed.

Eyebrows furled, lips tight, she pivoted and looked for me over the roof of the car. The air was grey and the orange street-lights hadn't come on yet. I had bent over my hand, fumbling for the leash, doggie treats and water in the back seat. I could never get the damn front seat to pop forwards easily.

'You don't see him?' I asked, walking over to her.

At first, I didn't see him either. Ginger, Gary's dog, stood alone in the front yard of Gary's house. Like a torpedo her black body honed in on us. Lauren had opened the back door on her side and Ginger waddled over immediately, looking for food.

Lauren turned to me, a perplexed expression on her face. 'Who's this?'

'Ginger,' I said. 'Gary's dog.'

When Ginger heard our voices she stopped. Her eyes caught ours and she looked at us for a moment as if she realised she didn't know us. Her body language suddenly changed, she stopped stood still, studying us with a distant aloofness that seemed to say, *Wait a moment, I don't know you. Who are you?*

Lauren looked at Ginger, smiled at her and looked back at me. I was waiting, hoping Gary would come out and make the formal introductions.

'I forgot to mention Ginger,' I said, looking at Lauren, who reached into the back seat for a dog treat.

At this point I heard a dog bark behind a fence lined with century plants, then a chain rattle down a metal leash line. When I looked around the bark came from Gary's backyard. The white clouds above his house were disappearing fast and in the greying light the canal looked blurry.

Squinting, I looked for Chewy. Behind me I heard people walking by, heading for the bridge. They were almost ghosts. *Crap*, I thought, *we missed him*.

Looking around again I thought I saw him up on the embankment, wrapped low around the telegraph pole. He was faint and blurry in the fading light.

'Lauren,' I said, 'he's by the pole, the telegraph pole.'

'Where?' she asked, confused.

'Over there.' I pointed to the middle telegraph pole. I lightly touched her shoulder and stuck my left arm out at the middle pole. 'The pole high up on the embankment.'

'Oh yes,' she said. 'I see him.'

She started to walk towards Chewy and my fingers twined themselves tighter around the leash and the other plastic bag full of treats. My feet marched off obediently behind hers.

Chewy stood, his mouth open, head bowed a little. Then he yawned. Even in dim light he sniffed the air, trying, it seemed, to distinguish if he knew us: were our scents familiar? Had he forgotten our odours? Had he lost them somewhere in his roaming? Had he confused us with someone else? The next thing I knew, he backed off.

'Oh, he's big,' Lauren said. 'That's good, I love big dogs.'

She turned and smiled at me, squeezing my hand. Then she resumed walking towards him.

'You did good, honey, bringing me here.'

That was all I wanted – Lauren excited and smiling at me.

Chewy, smelling the chicken treats, came slowly down the embankment. He scuffled up little puffs of dirt as he walked and watched us intently. His tail was held high, absentmindedly thrashing the air.

Ten feet from the car on the asphalt Chewy stopped. When he did so, Lauren also stopped. She dropped to one knee, putting her hand out.

'Oh, he's beautiful,' she said, 'especially in this light.'

I started to move up next to her but Chewy nervously shifted his head sideways, moving it back and forth, and looked up the embankment over his shoulder. Then he turned to go back.

I stopped; he stopped. Ginger came closer, sniffing for a treat. I knelt down, skidding the treat bag along the asphalt over to Lauren. Ginger's head followed the bag.

'He's so skittish,' she said in a low, puzzled voice.

Our conversation stopped. We waited four or five minutes without talking, wondering what to do, afraid to move, thinking Chewy might panic and run off. I gave Ginger the one treat I had in my hand, then she waddled off over to the front yard. Chewy watched her. Finally, Chewy lay down on the street with his head on his paws, still eyeing us warily. He waited. *What were these people up to, anyway?*

Lauren picked up the treats and pulled out four or five. She held her hand full of treats out to Chewy.

His head perked up, his eyes widened. He looked over directly at Lauren as if sizing her up. *Treats, yes; strange person, no; deliciously smelling treats; quiet strange person... Chicken treats you love... Yummmmm!*

I didn't know what to do; Lauren didn't know what to do. We waited in the middle of the street in the gathering darkness. Finally, Lauren lowered her outstretched hand to her side. Then she reached forwards and spread the treats out in a line on the asphalt and stepped back a few feet.

If I were a dog, especially one living on the streets, this was an absolute no-brainer. Chicken bits in a row, red as lipstick sticks, and a strange woman pulling her hands away from them, I thought. Chewy just looked at her. I would swear I saw him squint.

'This is going to be hard,' she said, looking at me. 'Poor guy, he really needs help.'

Lauren thought he appeared to be relatively healthy, just looking at him, but who knew what his true condition was? He must be lonely, terribly lonely. Dogs are pack animals. He's alone except for Ginger.

But he's just perfect.

Lauren didn't say it out loud, but she had fallen in love with Chewy. He was her kind of dog – a big dog. Beautiful. Shy. Gentle.

She wanted to rescue him now, right now.

That's why we had so many animals, Lauren thought. *I'm a sucker for animals, particularly animals in need. Heck, any animal, period. Once a needy guy crosses my path, I'm a marshmallow. Just gotta help those guys.*

Her mind was sparkling with possibilities. First, the rescue, then neutering him, then bringing him home. He'd be OK with the cats and great for Emma. The house was big enough. This was going to be perfect, just perfect.

'We have to help him,' Lauren said, smiling at me.

I knew that look, and I knew what was coming next – the charm offensive first, her voice turned sweet. 'Honey,' it began. Then the soft hand on my shoulder, Lauren's eyes looking deeply into mine, me buffeted with all her arguments about saving animals. So I offered a great first solution before she started in. The truth of the matter was that this time it would not take much for Lauren to convince me to bring a rescue into our household: I knew I was already enamoured with this big, beautiful dog.

'Let's go talk to this woman Cecelia,' I said. 'She's already helping him by feeding him and trying to gain his trust. Let's see what she has to say. Perhaps we could join forces.'

Join forces we did.

Lauren waved goodbye to Chewy eating his treats and in the darkness we drove the five blocks to Cecelia's house. Before I was up the first step, Lauren had knocked on her door.

Driving up, Lauren knew Cecelia was definitely an animal person. Wooden outdoor furniture tastefully piled with cat beds, big red food bowls and shiny water containers; a sign that said 'Max' and one that read 'Dog is my co pilot'. She guessed there were probably at least two dogs living in this house. Already she liked this Cecelia.

Cecelia's sister opened the door and invited us in. Cecelia walked in from the kitchen, wiping her hands on her apron. She was dressed in a grey skirt, white blouse and pull-over patterned sweater. Her curly hair was cut short and streaked with grey back over her ears. She had a big open smile on her face.

'I'm Cecelia,' she said, 'and this is my sister, Charlotte.'

Charlotte excused herself and went back into the kitchen. Three mixed-breed dogs were barking at our feet and one of them – Max, the bigger one – jumped up at me. He was trying to hump my leg.

'Oh, Max,' Cecelia said, 'stop that. You're so rude!' She shooed Max away. He retreated five feet, looking at me, and immediately came barking right back.

'Max, if this is the way you're going to behave we'll have to put you in the bedroom.'

Her harsh tone and stare stopped Max barking. He backed off to the other side of the living room, jumped up on the couch and put his paws over his ears, turning his head away, pouting.

'Don't mind him,' Cecelia said. 'He takes a while to quiet down but he's a lover.'

She turned to me. 'I didn't expect to see you so quickly. I've been thinking about our conversation we had earlier about Chewy, so I'm happy to see you.'

Cecelia then turned to Lauren and said, 'So you've seen him? Isn't he special?'

She waved her hands in the air and her eyes widened. Lauren's eyes widened and when Cecelia lowered her hands, Lauren took them in hers. I thought they were going to jump up and down like teenage girls talking about their boyfriends. Jon Katz has written about a vast network of animal lovers. It struck me that he was right, and Lauren and Cecelia were lifelong members. Empathy and caring were in their genes. Looking at the gleam in their eyes, I knew these two were animal soul sisters, listening to their siren song, pushovers for kittens and stray dogs. And I was going to be recruited.

Lauren and Cecelia chatted away excitedly about Chewy. Their bodies nodded, 'Yes, yes,' to each other in slow motion and I couldn't hear a word they said. It was as if they were in a silent movie and I was watching. I looked over at Max and he was staring at them wide-eyed and glued to their movements. I wanted to ask if he knew what was up but I thought he was probably still mad at me for not letting him hump my jeans.

· They were so animated, so excited I thought maybe they would launch into the air like rockets. Finally, calming down a bit, they sat down and turned to me and said: 'So, Bruce, what do you think?'

What do *I* think? I didn't know what I thought except that the phrase 'sisterhood is powerful' was so true. Lauren sat looking at me, her hands in her lap, smiling like she was hanging on my every word. Cecelia looked at Lauren for a moment and then looked at me and smiled. The Chewy rescue team was forming right before my eyes – Chewy's Magna Carta.

Then Cecelia said, 'Yes, Bruce, what do you think?' The sweet warmth in her voice so surprised me that inside my mind I knew any defences I had were already broached. I saw the drawbridge come down, the doors to the castle open. All I had to do was surrender. That's when I heard Lauren say, 'Here's the plan…'

We're committed to getting Chewy off the streets. Cecelia will feed Chewy in the morning, Bruce and I will feed him in the evening. We will bring extra treats and try and befriend Chewy so he will begin to trust us. We will try to get Chewy into our car, or even better, try to get him to follow us home. Simple, straightforward plans. Chewy will fall in love with us, for sure. How could he not? It is obvious he wants a home. Why else would he follow so many people home to their houses, if he did not want a home?

Lauren paused, looked wide-eyed at me and tightened her lips in emphasis.

If we were successful, Lauren and I would provide Chewy with a home. Since Cecelia already had three dogs she told us that night she did not feel she could provide a home for Chewy. Her original intent was to find Chewy a home. It made sense for us to take him in. Most likely he'd have no problem with Emma, and we'd see about our cats. Since Lauren was going to have surgery in a couple of months, which would require six to eight weeks recovery, we had to get this plan going soon.

No problem, Lauren thought. *We should be able to get Chewy off the streets and integrated into our family in a month, piece of cake.*

Little did we know how naïve our scheme was for we did not realise just how smart and scared Chewy really was.

Chapter Five

Lauren Wants a Dog

Three a.m. Moonlight glistened on the white sheets. A small hand pushed them back. Two eyes blinked. Frizzy brown hair popped from under the covers as Lauren Lee Parrill, aged seven, on her mission, slipped from the covers into her flip-flops and tiptoed across the room to her dresser.

Her parents, her two sisters and her cat, Toby, slept; the house on Albany Avenue was quiet. The entire block in Modesto, California was quiet except for the hum of traffic outside in the distance.

Lauren, a black silhouette against the dim moonlight, bent down and quietly pulled out a box from under her bed.

She thought for a moment whether she dare flick on the light and then decided not to. On the rug she lifted out the top two white folded towels and took out her hidden drawing pad, crayons and scotch tape. Then she stood up, gently pushed the box under the bed and pulled open the door to the hallway. She walked a few steps down the hallway and disappeared into the bathroom. On the cold linoleum floor, she spread out her paper and crayons. Quietly, but focused and determined, she scrawled out in big letters: 'I want a dog', the 'I' with the red crayon. With the blue, then the yellow, green and black, she printed 'want' in large letters. Then a purple 'A' and finally, all in red, 'DOG' in capitals. She went over the word 'DOG' three times, pressing hard.

'I want a DOG,' it read.

With her best artistic skills she drew a puppy and a happy face, labelling the face 'me'. Below the puppy she wrote 'My Dog'.

She looked up to see her face smiling at herself in the bathroom mirror. Everything was going according to her plan. Then she crayoned two more signs: 'I want a DOG' on both of them. She wasn't sure if this would work. Her father was pretty adamant about not getting a dog.

She put her crayons back in their box, one by one, careful they were straight and pushing them down hard so the crayon tip wouldn't be crushed by the stiff flap as she closed it tight. Then she put the crayons and her paper back in the box in her room. She picked up her secret messages and the scotch tape with her left hand, pushed the box holding her supplies under her bed with her big toe and opened the bedroom door leading into the hallway and living room.

No one was up yet. The house was still. Except for the hum of the refrigerator the kitchen was quiet. Triumphant, she walked down the hallway, through the living room into the kitchen and stood before the refrigerator door. She taped up her sign. Four pieces of scotch tape, one piece diagonally across each corner, rubbed down tight by the fleshy palm of her hand. Centred high up on the door so her mom and dad could clearly read her message in the morning.

She hung the other two secret messages: one from the fireplace in the living room, the other in the bathroom. No one could miss them.

Happy, she snuck back into bed and fell asleep. Her sisters never woke up. Mom and Dad were still asleep. In the morning she just knew when she woke up there would be a big YES to greet her.

She was right, of course. This was her third attempt in a campaign that lasted three months to convince her parents to get her a dog. After her first attempt, her dad had said, 'What are we going to do about her?' She had heard her mom and dad discussing dogs and daughters. The second attempt was met with silence.

This time, when she came into the kitchen early the next morning, her mom looked up from pouring milk at the kitchen table and said, 'What are we going to do with you, Lauren, dear?'

Lauren stood in the kitchen doorway, frowning. She didn't know whether to cry or pout.

When she heard her mother say, 'Oh, I suppose a new dog wouldn't be so bad,' she screamed and ran through the kitchen past her dad at the refrigerator, past her mom pouring milk, out the archway that led to the living room, past her older sister in the bathroom brushing her teeth and jumped up on her bed in the bedroom, screaming. 'YES, YES, YES! she screamed joyously. Then she jumped down, ran through the front room and back into the kitchen.

Her dad was waiting by the refrigerator to catch her in his arms.

She had never been so happy.

* * *

Lauren was an animal person at birth. She is an animal person now, and a dog person in particular. Always she has had a dog, or wanted one. 'I want a dog' isn't the first sentence she uttered but close to it. On our first date, I bumped up against the same determination that got her a dog as a child. I learned three things: the first two Lauren told me assertively. The third became very evident. Here's how it happened.

'Do you want to have dinner?' Lauren said, leaning against a big painting of mine. We were in the Artists' Gallery in Fort Mason, San Francisco, where she worked. It was a Saturday. The gallery handled my paintings. When she asked, I didn't know what to say: she was beautiful, and young. I was thirteen years older than her, a starving artist, and wondered why she would want to date me.

'Sure,' I said, hesitantly.

The date was at her apartment in San Rafael for dinner. Nervous, I was of course. Bring flowers, wear a suit and tie? Casual clothes? What would we talk about? I was out of practice. She was so much younger. I managed to turn up two hours late for our first date.

But that wasn't the worst part.

After a delicious homemade dinner, we were talking on her couch with two small cushions safely between us. Lauren's cat, Ben, sat on top of the cushions eyeing me warily. Lauren took my hands in her lap and looked directly into my eyes – I was worried.

'Look,' she said, 'I want two things: to get married and to have children. If you don't want either, don't waste my time. I'm through with jerks!'

I might be a jerk, I thought, *but I didn't want her to be through with me.* I'd never had a woman talk to me like that. Her eyes, firm but soft, looked directly into mine. I smiled as best I could, nodded my head and mumbled something that passed for agreement.

Just then Ben moved. He lifted one paw, stretched his rib cage, arched his spine, looked at me and walked off along the top of the couch. That didn't feel like a vote of confidence and I needed one. Then I lifted the two cushions he'd been sitting on to scoot closer to Lauren. When I did so, I learned the third thing about Lauren.

There was a wiggling lizard with its tail half chewed off, lying on the couch between us. The cat had dropped a little hunting trophy for Lauren to prove how masterful a hunter he was.

Disbelief and squeamishness doesn't cover my response. *What kind of message was this?* I thought. I was worried about an animal conspiracy against me. I knew that was nuts but this was the San Francisco Bay Area after all.

Lauren saw me dumbfounded, staring at the wiggling trophy.

'Oh,' she said in her no-nonsense style. 'Ben does that all the time.'

Nonchalantly she picked up the trophy, walked out onto her porch, pitched the lizard into the high weeds and sat back down next to me. Just then, Ben strolled over and sat back down on the couch again. He began purring for his praises.

It was then that I realised whatever else this woman was, she was an animal lover, and that animals were about to enter my life.

I'm not naturally an animal person – or at least I wasn't at that point. Oh, I'd had pets – tropical fish and turtles. I even raised praying mantas for a Boy Scout merit badge (I was an Eagle Scout). But my interest was mostly curiosity and scientific. I never formed deep personal emotional attachments to my pets; Lauren did.

Not that Lauren's life with animals had been plain sailing. When she was in her twenties, living on unfenced acreage near the Feather River Canyon close to Paradise, California, she'd managed a natural healthfood store. Her mixed-breed husky named Shilo and her purebred

Siberian Husky (Japala) loved to roam. And they had plenty of unfenced land to roam in. When Lauren went to work, the dogs went roaming. Both breeds potentially kill cats as prey and some of Lauren's neighbours began complaining. Lauren thought Japala had begun killing chickens. Twice the dogs returned home with mouths full of porcupine quills. Lauren tried tying them up. Driving home down the dirt road leading to the front porch of the house she lived in, Lauren would see Japala's one blue eye shining in the dark like a small candle and she'd hear Japala howl. Eventually she realised she was not prepared for two young huskies and particularly not for the high-maintenance, strong-willed dogs that huskies can sometimes be. She found someone to adopt Shilo, but Japala simply disappeared. One night she didn't come home. Most likely she was shot by one of Lauren's neighbours for killing chickens.

After that heartbreaking experience Lauren waited twenty years before getting another dog. She felt enormous guilt that Japala had paid the price for her ignorance and irresponsibility. Before getting another dog she needed to know she was mature and responsible enough for dog ownership.

She did, however, have cats. Cats were more self-sufficient and required less maintenance. When Lauren and I met and married three years later she was thirty-six and I was forty-nine. Lauren wanted children, as she'd asserted on our first date. She had always assumed she would have children but age and Nature worked against her. Trying to conceive ended after five years of unsuccessful infertility treatments, and Lauren and I finally accepted that we were not going to have children.

Grieving such a loss takes time. After a difficult year, it was cats that helped Lauren – or one cat in particular. She'd thought it would be fun to have kittens running around the house and she decided to become a foster mom to kittens – a foster mom would be an interesting and time-consuming adventure. Lauren began trapping cats and kittens with a non-profit making organisation based in the East Bay. She trapped cats in downtown office buildings, in abandoned houses and most excitingly, at the Oakland Airport.

Leo came into our lives from the airport. A very thin, skittish grey tabby, she found him sitting inside a trap, sadly staring out at her and her colleague. Leo, as Lauren named him, has markings that resemble a large wild cat – beautiful red/rust stripes scattered over his thin body, a raccoon-like tail, dark with grey circles – sweet but still skittish. He brought Lauren back to life. Twelve years later, Leo is still part of our household.

For years, I was merely a companion to Lauren's animal passion. Oh, I walked our dog, Emma, petted the cats and supported Lauren's passion for animals, but I never really thought or felt much about animals as separate beings. The first animal who began to change my mind was our neighbourhood free-thinking cat named Morris.

I'm a very tactile person – touching and touch is one of the important ways I learn about the world and about myself. Morris was a cat whose fur I simply loved: cuddling him, stroking him, burying my nose in his fur gave me great pleasure. Why, I don't really understand. Lauren would say, 'Because he's adorable, you dummy!'

Morris was an orange Manx tabby with thick, scrumptious fur. He was a neighbourhood cat who chose where he lived each night from among five or six houses, regularly returning to each for food and human companionship. After a year of bestowing visits upon us, Morris decided he would accept our house as his home. I was dead set against this because by this time we had Emma and five cats, but over time his extraordinary personality seduced me. As the king of the neighbourhood cats, Morris was fiercely independent, proud and regal but there was one tawdry habit he had that had me fall for him.

One day, sitting at my desk looking out our front window, I saw Morris in all his splendid orange tabbiness sauntering across the street. His short, stubby Manx tail and his hips, along with his furry pantaloon legs were swaying back and forth, looking for adventure. Morris climbed up the sidewalk on the left side, hid behind the first colonial column supporting the neighbour's front porch. He paused looking into the tall thin glass panel framing the front door. When he saw the neighbour's large dog moving inside the house, he slid sideways past the second column, crept up against the right side of the tall, thin glass panel. Then he stretched out full length very deliberately with his furry tummy facing the window and the dog. He then sat before the glass window intently and deliberately looking in at the dog. The expression on his face was most likely smiling, as if to say, 'Come and get me you big brute! Hee, hee, you can't.'

The dog went ballistic. Throwing himself against the glass, again and again. He was barking, growling so loud that I could easily hear him across the street. After a minute or a minute and a half of this frenzied barking, Morris stepped out of view. I'm sure the dog knew he was still there – he could probably smell him. The dog agitated, rocking hard back and forth on his front paws, head scanning right and left, searched for Morris. But after a brief period the dog quieted himself, and wandered off into the interior of the house. Just as he did, Morris swished his body in front of the window and, not getting the response he wanted, sat down directly in front of the window again.

And the dog ran back and lunged at the window. I could hear him across the street.

Morris sat unflappable. He leaned forwards and began licking his front left paw as if he had nothing more important to do in the world. The dog went into spasms of throwing himself at the window. Bang, bang, bang! He threw his body at the glass. Sitting at my desk, I worried he'd break it. So much so that in the next few days I informed the dog's owners about what

I'd seen. They seemed unconcerned – they didn't put their dog in their backyard, nor pull the curtain across the glass window.

Not every day, nor every week, but a couple of times a month Morris sauntered across the street for his fun and entertainment. When Lauren noticed him taunting the neighbour's dog she would always go over and grab Morris and take him back home. This did not deter Morris. I understood that her doing this was being responsible, perhaps even being fair and just, but the adolescent twelve-year-old inside of me that drives much of my behaviour rooted for Morris and enjoyed watching him. After being deterred by Lauren, he would just wait a few days to try again. And when the dog was sufficiently lathered, Morris simply pivoted on his haunches and walked away.

I know that it is shameless to admire Morris's behaviour. Perhaps it means I'm emotionally immature (most likely I am). But I liked Morris all the more for it, and when he was hit and killed by an automobile, I was inconsolable for two days. I was surprised by the depth and complexity of my feelings. Holding his dead body in my arms, I cried unashamedly. Even now, writing this, my eyes are filling up.

Chewy was the second animal to deeply touch me. Not all at once but slowly, as if he were revealing himself to me. First, his beauty transfixed me. The image of him cantering up the street, young and carefree, haunted me.

Then his gentleness drew me in, his joyous play with other dogs, how gingerly he approached people, his careful soft mouth when eating – all spoke of something deeper. Or so I imagined.

I was hooked.

Chapter Six

They Had No Right
to Shoot Chewy

They shot Chewy.

Gary heard them shoot Chewy.

Within seconds, the maximum impact, 40-gram less-than-lethal 'bullet bean bag' smashed into Chewy's side.

Gary was furious now. They had no right to shoot Chewy, no right at all. In fact, they had shot him twice: once in the left hip socket, and once just below his rib cage.

Terrified, Chewy ran. Gary watched him disappear up Enslen Street. He ran like a runaway freight train. A straight, powerful full force, panting frantically, perhaps crying out, his head glancing back over his shoulder, eyes wide open in terror. Before his adrenaline failed him, he'd run at least three quarters of a mile through traffic and across two streets and disappeared into the distance.

In the warm afternoon sun, he would have run to where he felt safest. Perhaps under a dumpster, perhaps into the basement of an abandoned house or simply, he might have crawled under some local bush and hid with his back against a fence, his whole body shaking, where most pedestrians would never see him.

While we don't know where he hid, we do know that he wouldn't have understood why they shot at him.

* * *

Cecelia said she'd seen the officers circling only days before the shooting happened. They were just two decent guys, doing their job protecting the citizens of Modesto from dangerous strays. He was that big red dog by the canal bridge someone had complained about; they were looking for him. Circling in their patrol car, checking for him, they'd seen that big red dog by the canal.

Cecelia had seen their black-and-white patrol car drive by the canal. Then minutes later, the two officers drove by again, only slower. Cecelia was at Gary's house, ready to feed Chewy. She saw the animal control officers circling the park a third time.

Were they looking for Chewy? *You bet they are*, Cecelia told herself. Chewy, where was Chewy? 'Chewy! Chewy!' Cecelia shouted in a low whisper. She didn't want to alert the officers; she wanted Chewy down by her, below the crest of the canal embankment where the officers couldn't see him. She would keep him safe.

Drawn by the scent of chicken breasts, he'd come down from the telegraph pole to the bushes near the electrical substation.

'Oh, there you are, Chewy! My wonderful little angel…' Cecelia talked to him, encouraging him to stay hidden there so the officers would not see him. It worked.

Cecelia walked to the base of the canal bridge. Oops, there they were! She spun around abruptly, and hid back in the bushes with Chewy. He just looked at her. Five minutes later she checked again: still there. On the third check, the patrol car was gone. It had been over a half hour since Cecelia had first seen them. *They've gone someplace else*, she hoped.

She tried to give Chewy a big kiss on his forehead but he backed away. 'We're going to rescue you somehow,' she told him. 'I'm sure of that. My good Mr Chewy.'

After a year and a half on the streets, sometimes running with other strays, sometimes not, Chewy had probably seen stray dogs caught by animal control. He would have witnessed how they struggled and never came back. Chewy had outsmarted everyone trying to catch him, well-intentioned people wanting to rescue him, with food in one hand and a collar in the other. Now the two officers were back.

The afternoon he was shot, Chewy watched them with Gary. He heard the human noises they were making; he understood loud, harsh sounds. Sharp, quick movements scared him.

We can imagine the tone of their argument put him on alert.

'Is that your dog?' the officer said.

'What if he is my dog?' Gary answered.

'He's off-leash, sir.' Gary glanced quickly at the tall officer and then swung around to see the smaller officer lock and load the 12-gauge shotgun (the 12-gauge was pointed at the ground). The taller officer said: 'We got a complaint, he's scaring people.'

'*Chewy?* He's not scaring anyone,' Gary said angrily. 'He's more afraid of them.'

'Well, sir, we got a complaint. We're going to scare him off. Please stand back.' He motioned to the smaller officer.

'You can't shoot Chewy!' Gary said. He took a step towards the officers. Then Chewy heard the cracking explosion and felt the hot flash whack his left side and another hit his rear. Both shots knocked him backwards six inches, almost to the ground. Chewy panicked.

The force of a bean-bag shot at twenty feet can knock a grown man down. Chewy was only four stone something, three-quarters his normal weight. He was a young dog, not a mature adult; he was hit with bean-bag bullets designed to shock and immobilise humans.

Many US police departments have rescinded the use of bean-bag ammunition – not all, but many. They're worried about lawsuits from collateral damage. So much so that departments' standard procedures include documenting each discharge.

After Chewy was shot, he crawled away and hid. If he'd been hit straight on, he would probably have been barely able to walk but he was lucky.

'Just days later,' Gary said, 'he was standing back by the telegraph pole – I couldn't see any visible damage.'

* * *

'We'd better get going,' Lauren said, sensing the situation was painful for Gary to recount.

'But they shouldn't have shot Chewy.' The anger came back into his voice. 'There was no need, he wasn't hurting anyone – I told them there were good people wanting to adopt and rescue Chewy. You know what they said? They said people had been complaining about a big red dog hanging out near the bridge. Could you believe that?'

We could. We didn't want to, but we could. As we talked, we knew some people were just scared of dogs. Any dogs. Others had bad experiences with big dogs. Chewy had followed people home. Always at a safe distance but he had followed them for blocks. That scared some people, especially women with babies in strollers. If I were a new mother, I'd be scared. We could understand that situations get complex: judgement requires perspective.

Gary was also looking after Chewy and trying to protect him. In his mid-fifties or so, Gary has the appearance of someone living in the mountains or a contractor. Usually in jeans, a plaid shirt and work boots, you can tell he has worked hard all of his life. He has had his troubles, like all of us but he has a gentleness of heart beneath his rugged exterior.

I myself had seen people scared by Chewy when he was still on the streets. While walking the neighbourhood for exercise on the way to see my beautiful dog, a young woman pushing a baby stroller across the street shouted to me: 'Is that your dog?'

There was concern in her voice. 'He's been following me for two blocks,' she added.

'No,' I said, then saw Chewy. I crossed over the street and clapped my hands. Chewy backed up.

'Here, boy,' I said. 'How you doing?' I leaned forwards. He backed up, turned away and looked at me over his shoulder. Then he trotted in the opposite direction down the street, turned right and disappeared.

'He's very gentle,' I told the woman.

'You think he's gentle?' she said.

'Well, he just took off. He greets people at the bridge up the street – he never barks or bites.'

'I hope you're right,' she said, walking away.

Some people just don't know, or trust, dogs.

But Gary knew one thing for sure: there was no need to shoot Chewy. Chewy wasn't hurting anyone. No way!

Chapter Seven
A Surprise, So Close

'When will we ever get Chewy off the streets?' Lauren asked. We were sitting in our living room.

She sounded wounded. Her face was flushed, red and puffy, almost in tears. We had been watching *The Blind Side*, the movie where a spunky Sandra Bullock saves Michael Oher from ghetto poverty. He ends up playing college football on a scholarship and then gets to play professional football.

'We have to get Chewy off the streets,' Lauren said. Her voice hardened on 'we' and 'get'; tears were near. I knew what that meant: desperation had set in. The movie hadn't helped. Now, she was focused. 'We', meaning she and I, had a mission: if Sandra could save Michael from street life, we could save Chewy from a stray's life, from being shot at in the street.

* * *

After six weeks of feeding Chewy every night, we were making some progress but it was slow. Chewy was still nervous. We continued to try and win him over. After feeding him, each night after dark, we would get in the car and turn on the headlights. Chewy would be sitting in the middle of the road staring at us with sad eyes as we drove away. *Where are you going? Why can't I come with you?* his look seemed to convey. It was heartbreaking, night after night, not to bring him home with us; also incredibly frustrating! It felt like he wanted to come with us and not be left alone in the dark. But he could not bring himself to make that last step in trusting us.

We thought if, when we get to sixteen weeks of feeding Chewy he still didn't trust us, then we must try sixteen more weeks, and sixteen more. Sooner or later, we'd break through. Yes, he'd followed us from Gary's house part of the way home, tail wagging, but something always stopped him. Was it just shyness? Had Modesto's mean streets soured him on humans? It didn't matter: if we just tried harder, paid attention to his needs, he'd bond with us eventually. Lauren was convinced of this but I wasn't so sure.

One weekend while walking Emma, we visited Chewy on our way home. After spending some time with him, we started walking down the canal bank towards our house.

Chewy started following us! Lauren and I were so excited. Maybe it would be tonight that he would come home with us. Wouldn't that be fantastic? We were both excited and nervous, but we knew we had to act nonchalantly. He kept following us, walking some twenty feet behind us on the crest of the canal ridge. The sun was setting behind him. Lauren kept turning round to see if he was still there. 'He's still following us!' she whispered to me as if I hadn't looked.

Her body had the energy of a rambunctious two-year-old: excited and barely able to contain herself.

After a few blocks we approached Sycamore Avenue.

'You think he'll cross?' I queried.

The street is only two lanes but it goes over the canal so it is an access street and very busy.

When we got to the street, Chewy tagged along up to the sidewalk. Then he stopped. Both Lauren and I were nervous: we didn't want Chewy hit by a car. Unleashed, we had no control over his actions. We waited until there was a larger break in traffic and then we pretended to casually walk across the street. But Chewy would not cross. We tried coaxing him, to no avail. For whatever reason he decided it was not safe to cross the street and follow us home. Maybe he picked up on our nervousness and decided we were still not safe enough for him.

'I'll try again,' I said. I walked back across the street as dusk darkened the sky. Chewy was like a ghost, a mirage on the horizon standing back on the canal bank.

'Come on, boy,' I said repeatedly. I walked out into the middle of the street under the street-lights. A car was coming. I held out my arms to stop it.

The car slowed. Chewy had backed up – I realised he wasn't going to cross the street. I stepped back on the kerb on Chewy's side of the street, looking back at

Lauren and shrugged my shoulders in the darkness. We tried several more times. Eventually, we gave up and shooed him back in the direction we had come so he would go back to Gary's and be safe.

Somehow we had to come up with another solution to get Chewy off the streets.

* * *

The next Saturday, at Gary's house, Chewy approached wide-eyed and head cocked, sniffing as he approached us like an old friend. Lauren bent down and put her hand out, palm up. Instinctively Chewy backed away. I watched from the middle of the street. What was going on? What did it take with this dog? His backing away was maddening and confusing. Were we doing something wrong? Some little thing that The Dog Whisperer, Cesar Millan, could easily correct? 'See,' Cesar would say in his gentle voice, 'See, just do this,' and Chewy would be licking and kissing us.

Lauren tried again, talking to Chewy softly – 'Chewy, Chewy, you handsome boy. How are you today? What a beautiful doggie!' Chewy inched forwards, head lifted, tail wagging.

I walked back over to Lauren's car and opened the back door. Of course I understood Chewy's jumping into the back seat was hopelessly unrealistic. Chewy was smart, very smart. Living on the street had honed his wits – his street survival sense. But perhaps some miracle might happen, like Lassie jumping into the back seat of the family wood-sided station wagon and off they drive, one happy family.

When the car door opened, he looked up curious, staring in from a safe distance. But he did not jump in: he knew this game. Instead he walked away and lay down by his telegraph pole, staring at us. 'Really,' his eyes seemed to say, 'you'll have to do better than that. I'm not falling for that old trick – I've been around the block a few times.'

Since he'd been seen on the streets as a puppy, running with stray dogs, it meant he'd lived on the streets for probably a year and a half. He ran loose, scrounged for food, dodged traffic and slept under bushes. Of course fear took hold. Poor Chewy, no wonder he was scared. People trying to trick him or catch him, or even shoot him. Why wouldn't he be shy and skittish? But we feared if the local animal control caught him, and sooner or later they would, he'd most likely be put down. We drove back home confused about what to do.

Lauren was beginning to panic. It was mid-December and she had a major operation scheduled for mid-January.

Lauren is a no-nonsense person but she had a physical problem. She had developed large benign tumours and required surgery to remove them. Also, she had a genetic predisposition to cancer from her father, which was increased by her having taken infertility drugs for several years, so her scheduled surgery would provide immediate relief from the physical pain caused by the tumours and relieve her worry that she might develop ovarian cancer. Surgery it was.

Three days in the hospital and six to eight weeks lying in bed at home. We didn't have enough time to socialise Chewy before her operation. Bonding takes time, you couldn't socialise him in three weeks. Not even Cesar could do that! *Get serious*, Lauren thought. Rescue might have to wait until after her operation and recovery but that was three months away. She'd go nuts worrying about Chewy. Who would feed him in the evenings? What if animal control caught him, or a car hit him? Chewy might not survive.

* * *

Many people view pets as property, easily disposed of as they wish. Thankfully, most people acting responsibly find their pets homes or simply take them to Animal Control. In our neighbourhood strays, dumped or simply escaped, appeared sporadically. Wandering the streets or trotting along the canal, desperate for food, seeking attention, sometimes scaring people, mostly they were curious. My impulse was always to rescue them.

Over the years I'd seen so many abandoned dogs I carried a spare leash in my truck. Even before Chewy, I'd brought two dogs home myself.

Sam, an energetic reddish-brown part Lab and part Siberian mix, knocked on the front door screen with his nose, hungry and rambunctious. Before I could get a leash on him, he ran across the street to explore a neighbour's front porch. When I opened our front gate, in he came. *Oh boy, oh boy, a big new yard and cats*! He went wild, chasing our cats. Up in the trees they went hissing. Sam was a frenzy of barking and jumping. Our choice was clear: we adopted him out to a farmer with a lot of land for him to roam.

But Buster, a labradoodle, I simply loved. I don't understand why but then again I fall so easily, so quickly. Buster did what I loved: he climbed up into my lap as if he knew me all his life. He put his paw on my leg when he wanted attention; he chased every ball I threw, and dropped it at my feet, barking for more. He licked my chin and jumped up on me like I was a puppy magnet. Was I a soft touch? You bet! Why? Who cared? I just enjoyed it.

Fortunately for Buster, but unfortunately for us, a young blonde-haired woman called and came over after seeing our flyer advertising we had found him. I hinted that if Buster was too much trouble we would gladly take him. 'No, that was fine,' she said. Buster was elated to go back home – seems he periodically escaped. Buster's big adventure was following scents, wandering the streets, playing with new dogs he met in the local park until someone finally caught him and brought him home.

'It happens all the time,' his owner said. 'He's sneaky and smart. He can dig under any fence. He hides where you don't see him and then psisssh – he's gone!'

I loved his energy. A labradoodle, I told myself, that would be the next dog after Chewy. I'd name him Henry. He'd be chocolate brown mix with curly hair and endless energy.

But Chewy was different. The hard, mean streets had taught him to be careful and cagey: people had to earn his trust. Neither Cecelia feeding him in the morning, nor Lauren and I feeding him in the evening was social-ising him. He allowed us to pat his head. He'd sniff a hand momentarily and then quickly back away after snatching food from our hands, but nothing more. No hugs or petting. No jumping up into the front seat of our car, excitedly panting, *Take me home, take me home, guys!* No following Lauren down the canal and over the foot-bridge to our house, eager to scramble up the front steps in through our front door and cuddle up on the couch to watch Sandra Bullock save Michael Oher – none of that for Chewy. Yet his beauty, shyness and the particularly gentle way he delicately lifted food from our hands led Lauren and I to believe he would work out just fine in our house. We simply had to get him *to* our house.

We didn't know what to do. At night Lauren lay awake, trying to figure him out. 'Do you think he'll be OK with our cats?' she'd say.

'What?' I'd ask groggily, rolling over on my pillow in the darkness to look at her. *This is the woman I love*, I'd think.

'Sure,' I'd say, 'Can we sleep now?'

Chewy's behaviour was driving Lauren in particular, and me in support, nuts. She couldn't figure him out, nor could anyone else.

Then one Friday night she said, 'I've got it! Let's try Emma.'

Emma would befriend Chewy and he would follow her home. At this time Emma was around eleven years old. She was another rescue dog, whom we adopted when she was a puppy from a rescue group in Marin County. This group would travel to the Lake County animal shelter, north of Marin County, and take adoptable dogs that were close to being euthanised. Emma was part Lab, German shepherd and pit bull... we think. A wonderful, loving dog, she was fierce with those she did not know, though.

Lauren brought Emma with us to Gary's house. Chewy immediately sniffed Emma, licked her and started to play. He put his paws up on Emma's back, barking in an invitation to play. Then he snapped at her, friendly dominance play. Emma backed away and looked at Chewy, letting out a low, sustained growl. She was slightly barring her teeth: who was dominant here, who was in control; who was this new dog, with all that energy?

I'm too old for this nonsense, Emma seemed to be saying. She walked away and lay down near our car. Lauren was frustrated. Chewy backed off. I sat down on the kerb and poured water into one of Chewy's water bowls, all the while thinking, *now what?*

Chapter Eight
Panic Sets In – Upping the Ante

That night Lauren had her second brainstorm: she called Mike O'Brien, our veterinarian. And we went to see him. Balding, mid-fifties, able to multi-task easily, Mike had all the energy needed to conquer the animal world, or at least that part of the dog world that encompassed Modesto. Say 'vet' and most animal owners in town think of Mike. His son Chad became a vet too. Together as business partners, they'd recently built a new low-waste, solar-powered, earth-friendly 'green' veterinary clinic.

Mike is amazingly dedicated to improving the lives of animals in our community. He helps provide free spaying and neutering clinics. Not only does the community receive free services, Mike offers vet students an opportunity to participate in the clinic to enhance their own firsthand experience. Through the local County Animal Shelter, he also participates in a non-profit-making organisation that offers similar services for low-income residents.

'Try a loop leash,' Mike suggested. The loop leash has a clip at one end and a loop-hole at the end that can be used as a handle – many veterinarian clinics, dog kennels and groomers use them. He gave us one.

'Yeah,' Mike said, 'Just lasso him, like a cowboy lassoing a cow.'

But we weren't cowboys, we didn't have a horse and Chewy wasn't a cow.

'I'm kidding,' Mike added, seeing our puzzled faces. 'Put the leash on the ground by your feet, or slip it over your arm, resting in your elbow. When feeding Chewy, quickly slip it over his head. No problem.'

It all sounded eminently simple. Mike mentioned if Lauren were successful, she would need to hold on tight to the leash. Once collared, Chewy would freak out, fight and try to pull away, or simply break free. Sixty pounds of frightened fighting St Bernard mix would be a handful, he warned, not to mention there being some risk of being bitten. *Wow, we never thought of that! This could get serious real quick*, Lauren thought.

Little did we know how true this would be...

Mike also planned for a worst-case scenario. 'If the leash doesn't work, we'll put tranquillisers in raw meat, like hamburger,' he said, smiling. 'That should knock him out.' He made that plan sound even easier: the food would knock him out and we'd take a snoring Chewy over to get tested, vaccinated and neutered. It was all very tidy and simple.

That all made sense, Lauren thought, but first she had to try the loop leash. Cecelia agreed. So did I. Loop leash first, medication second…

* * *

Next weekend Lauren was determined to try the loop leash. Saturday, when we arrived at Gary's house, Chewy was in the front yard with Ginger. Out of my backpack I took cooked chicken pieces, rolled doggy sausages and some dried chicken jerky. Lauren had lovingly prepared the chicken that morning. She sat down in Gary's yard and began cooing to Chewy (she had the loop leash with her). This time Chewy came over immediately. He let Lauren pet him on his head as she fed him treats. Ginger nudged Lauren's arm, smelling the chicken: she wanted her fair share. I sat across the street on the kerb, watching.

Chewy let Lauren pet his side. Rubbing him, Lauren said, 'I'm going to try.' She reached for the leash.

Chewy backed off, skittish by the movement. Then he came back closer again for more chicken. In the next few minutes, Lauren missed several opportunities to leash Chewy. Watching her was like watching the Chicago Cubs play baseball: missed opportunity after missed opportunity. Then I figured she knew what she was doing – after all, she was the one doing it, not me.

'I don't want to mess this up,' she said, still rubbing Chewy's head. Then quickly her hand picked up the leash and put it over Chewy's head. I couldn't believe it. Chewy was startled, stunned and motionless. Lauren reached over and pulled the loop tight at Chewy's neck so that the leash acted as a collar; his neck fur was thick. *Hold it tight*, she thought to herself. *Just hold tight*.

As Mike predicted, Chewy reacted quickly, *very* quickly. He jerked back. *What was this around my neck?* He jumped and pulled away suddenly. Lauren felt her arm being yanked, her heart pounding. Chewy's speed and strength surprised her. Looking down at her hand, she saw the leash slithering quickly through it. She gripped it more tightly but the rope kept sliding. *No, no*, Lauren thought, *hold on, don't mess this up*. Holding on took all of a second. Lauren saw the tail of the leash whip out of her hand.

She went to grab it with her other hand, but Chewy was quicker, his pull stronger than Lauren's. The moment the rope slipped out of her hand, Chewy was gone. *This can't be happening*, Lauren told herself.

Chewy ran up the canal, the leash around his neck, dangling beside him like a loose rope caught in his fur. Stunned, open-mouthed, Lauren collapsed onto the asphalt, watching. She wanted to scream 'No, no!' but she saw Chewy run over the canal bridge and towards the park. He covered 200 yards before Lauren jumped up. This was terrible; our worst nightmare had come true.

Lauren looked over at me. I was equally stunned. 'Chase him. For God's sake, chase him!' I yelled.

Maybe we could grab the leash, maybe someone else would, maybe it would get tangled in some bushes and then we could bring him back… But Chewy was running rapidly out of sight. *Oh God*, I thought, *he is so frightened, he will run into traffic and get killed*. I imagined a bleeding Chewy on the asphalt, his guts spilled all over the street. Chewy, whining on his side, legs kicking in the air as he attempted to get up.

'Chase him, chase him!' I yelled. Lauren seemed too stunned to move.

She looked at me like I was an idiot. 'Chase him? Chase him? Chewy's scared, you fool! Do you really think we're going to catch him?'

I didn't know what to think, nor did she but we needed to do something. Chewy with the leash wrapped around his neck might choke himself to death on bushes, or through some freak accident. But I was in no fit shape to run – I was a tortoise and Lauren was the hare – a fifty-two-year-old hare maybe but thirteen years younger than me and in better condition. Almost simultaneously, we looked at each other and realised between our two bad alternatives she was the only one who could run.

Off she went. What you must know about Lauren is that she hates to run. Leisure running might have been my exercise of choice but it was certainly not Lauren's. At fifty-two years of age, she hadn't run in thirty years yet there she was, a frumpy, grey-haired woman, at least twenty pounds overweight, chasing a beautiful, young, scared-to-death dog. In her Keen sandals she took off. She ran across gravel, up and down a small hill, over a bridge onto the sidewalk. Think Bette Middler running, think *Chariot of the Gods*, housewives edition.

As she ran some of our neighbours shouted support: 'Do you need help, dear?', 'He ran that way', 'Need a lift?' Other people simply stopped and stared: what was going on?

It didn't help that Lauren stopped every twenty-five yards and bent over, hands on knees panting, a sharp pain in her right side. Meanwhile Chewy ran like an expensive thoroughbred: graceful, fur flowing in the wind, long, even strides across the bridge, shooting through a small opening onto a grass lane, where he stopped and turned to see if that crazy woman was still following him.

Then Lauren saw him run across a busy two-lane street right into traffic without looking. A Prius just missed him. Screeching tyres. But Chewy was through traffic, on the other side of the street, like he knew the obstacle course.

He ran into Enslen Park across the street. Lauren could barely make him out ahead of her through the trees as she crossed the street into the park. Out of breath, doubled over in pain, she stopped. *Oh God*, she thought, *I'm losing him*. She took even, deep breaths and fumbled forwards.

'You go, girl!' a homeless woman yelled.

Chewy was at the other end of the park. He would periodically stop and look back, only to see that strange lady whom he had slightly trusted still running after him. *He's still scared*, Lauren thought, *and he's a lot faster than I am.*

Chewy kept going. He crossed a second street. *Chasing him isn't working*, Lauren thought. *It's only made things worse.* She got to a corner near a small neighbourhood grocery store. A group of people walking in the neighbourhood started shouting and pointing, 'He went that way, down the alley.' *I feel like I'm running the Bay to Breakers* [an annual footrace that takes place in San Francisco, California], she thought, *crowds cheering me on as I'm running up Heartbreak Hill.*

She looked up the street and caught a glimpse of Chewy's white-tipped tail as he turned left down the alley. Lauren stood and looked on in disbelief: Chewy was only half a block from our house. *What a shame*, she thought. She threw up her hands – all of this for nothing?

By the time Lauren reached the alley, she was walking defeated. Her breathing was normal, but her heart was crushed. Looking down the alley, she saw Chewy turning left at the end of it: he was making a loop. *What a smart dog – he's brilliant*, she said to herself, smiling. He was going back to the canal and back to Gary's house. Bruce was still at Gary's house. Maybe there was still some hope.

When she got there, exhausted and depressed, there was only Bruce.

'Have you seen him? Did he come back? He was headed this way.'

But Chewy was nowhere to be found. We waited awhile for him in the late afternoon. If only the loop leash had worked. If only this, if only that… It was too depressing.

After talking it over, we decided to drive around looking for Chewy. But he had vanished – hiding under bushes, gone into some secret dog place where no one would find him. After all, he was the expert at surviving on the streets.

Later that day towards dusk when we normally fed Chewy, Lauren and I went back to Gary's house, hoping Chewy would be there: he was not. We thought he might be gone for good. We went over to Cecelia's house to tell her the bad news.

'Oh no, not my Chewy!' Cecelia gasped.

Sitting in her living room, we were three depressed adults. 'Where do you think he's gone?', 'I hope he doesn't tangle himself up on some fence and strangle himself to death'… We thought the leash could get caught under a car tyre and Chewy would be dragged down the street. One after another dangerous scenario presented itself, all due to our well-intentioned but ill-executed attempt to rescue him. All of our efforts for two months had vanished, just like that.

* * *

The next day we went back to Gary's house and Gary was home.

'You what?' he said. We told him our story. He was strangely unaffected. 'Look,' he said, a sly smile on his face. 'Don't worry.'

Don't worry? I thought, *you must be nuts.*

'Don't worry about the leash,' Gary said, 'Chewy chewed it off.'

We both looked at him in disbelief.

'Yeah,' he said. 'I saw him yesterday evening, he was OK – he played with Ginger. He had this collar thing on him and I wondered where it came from.'

What a smart dog! No wonder he survived in the street a year and a half. We could relax, even sleep.

After a few days of going over to Gary's house in the hope of seeing Chewy again, we finally saw him. There he was, greeting people as they came over the bridge, or sitting by the telegraph pole near the canal bank as if nothing had happened. And he looked fine: he still had the loop leash around his neck with a small, chewed-off stub. He had bitten off the long tail of the leash. Thank goodness! What a smart dog, what a beautiful dog sitting in the sun.

The loop leash rescue had failed and he was wary of us again. He had outsmarted both of us, trying to catch him, but we weren't about to give up. Rescue plan one had failed. Now we respected him and his street smarts even more. Winter was here, bringing storms, rain and cold winds. Would Chewy even remain at Gary's? Might he decide to move on? If so, would we lose him?

Lauren's operation was just weeks away.

Chapter Nine
Time is Running Out

Dark thunderheads swirled over Modesto; clouds like heavy stones in the sky. Thunderstorms every few weeks meant cold days and even colder nights for Chewy. Winter storms cracked and blew tree limbs down; street gutters flooded and leaves clogged roof drains. Branches were scattered and blown across dark green lawns. After the second storm, our phone lines were knocked out for three hours. Two blocks away from us, the power lines were down. A utility truck rumbled down our alley, stopped, dropping three-legged prongs to steady the truck while repairmen clambered up poles with metal tools clanging off their hips. They moved like rock climbers.

By early January, when we went outside to feed Chewy, people walked holding their umbrellas tight against the wind. At the canal, Chewy's hole was a puddle. During late fall and winter the canals are dry: water from reservoirs feeds the land, after harvest is over; the flow of water stops and the land rests until the next season. The empty canal collected dirty puddles of water. The hundred-year-old century plant by Gary's fence was grey and beaten down. On Gary's grass lay soaked plaid blankets. Kibble left for Chewy was blown and scattered off the sidewalk. The wind had flipped over and blown up into the bushes a large plastic doghouse a neighbour had left for him to sleep in during the cold rainy nights.

Chewy was jumpy and frightened. He slept nights hunkered down among the bushes along the electrical substation wall or along Gary's fence. With each storm, getting soaked, each night standing by his telegraph pole, he looked more vulnerable, more frightened and hopeless. His fur stuck to his body in ugly matted clumps; his back leg hair was a muddy brown. His backside was plastered with small twigs; crushed leaves and clumps of mud hung from his behind. Soaked and quivering, he stared blankly out at people crossing the bridge in the light rain.

We had lost ground: he was more cautious of us. When we came to feed him, he watched Lauren's hands, his eyes tracking her fingers and his nose sniffing suspiciously. Skittish and hesitant, he backed away repeatedly until Lauren's soft gentle voice coaxed him back to daily feedings.

He'd had a week's reprieve before the next storm but after more than two months of daily feedings and coaxing, we were almost ready to give up. We were not progressing in our efforts to get him off the streets. *What will work? What haven't we done right?*, we asked ourselves. *What else could we try?* We were at a loss for new ideas. When the heavy rains came, both Lauren and

Cecelia were deeply concerned. Then Lauren's operation came and went.

'I can't take it anymore,' Cecelia said to her sister Charlotte, warm in their living room. 'Chewy's cold and soaking wet!'

Cecelia's voice was a mixture of despair, determination and hope. Her sister smiled to herself: she knew this meant another crusade.

'Let the chips fall where they may,' Cecelia exclaimed. Then she called Lauren.

Lauren heard the despair. In week one of a six-week recuperation from surgery, propped up by pillows in the bedroom, she looked at the ceiling. *Yes, yes, yes*, she thought, *we have to get him. You have to get him – he can't be out there in these storms. He's miserable.*

She told Cecelia: 'You're right, we have to do something. Another big storm is coming – Chewy will freeze.'

Lauren grimaced when she sat up. I put another pillow behind her back to make her more comfortable.

Cecelia outlined her plan, saying excitedly, 'I'm going to rescue him, this can't go on – I just can't stand it! I'm going to get tranquillisers from Mike and get him off the street.'

Lauren looked up at me and she started to mouth what Cecelia had said. She stopped herself mid-sentence and spoke out loud: 'Cecelia's going to rescue Chewy!'

I smiled. A few days after Lauren's operation, she was still on pain medication and confined to bed. Mostly, she slept and read mysteries as her energy came back. Cecelia had been feeding Chewy in the morning; I fed him in the evenings.

'You're right,' Lauren said into the phone. 'You're absolutely right. This can't go on!'

Lauren was jubilant. Nothing, she knew, absolutely nothing would deter Cecelia. She was so relieved – Chewy would be safe now. There were questions, of course. If Cecelia was successful and caught Chewy, then what would happen to him? Lauren couldn't take care of him right now, she could barely get out of bed, but we knew we'd figure these other questions out later. We'd come up with a plan that would work.

* * *

Cecelia laid the plastic bag with the five tiny yellow tranquillisers on her kitchen counter. They shone like little pearls in the fluorescent lights. In the kitchen next to her, Charlotte said, 'They're smaller than I imagined.'

Cecelia picked up the bag and held one pill between her fingers: she looked at it. Chewy must not smell them. She could imagine his black muzzle sniffing the small hamburger balls, his tongue licking them; she knew dogs had a sense of smell far superior to that of humans. Max, her Lhasa Apso, could smell anything.

'Maybe I ought to coat them with olive oil?' she said.

'Let's hope this works, you're spending an awful lot of time trying to get this dog,' Charlotte said, smiling and pulling open the refrigerator door. She checked the shelves and found the Sciabica grassy green olive oil, the best in Modesto – nothing too good for Chewy!

She liked its smell. Charlotte poured a small amount in a bowl, then formed the hamburger into small balls and dipped them in. Now they were coated in olive oil. There were five fragrant meatballs – quite a meal for a hungry dog. She cooked them while Cecelia got her leash and put on her deep blue sweatshirt. Once they were browned and cool, she pushed the pills one at a time into the five meatballs. Deep, so Chewy couldn't find or smell them. She licked her fingers.

By 6.30 p.m. Cecelia was ready to go. Her keys were by the kitchen door.

She and Mike guessed Chewy weighed about eighty pounds. Chewy looked healthy except for a little arthritis in his hips; he certainly played healthy. Neither Mike nor Cecelia had thought about an overdose risk. If anything, they worried they might err in giving him too little and that half-drugged, he'd wander out into the street and get hit by a car. Killing him accidentally was unaccept-able. Mike had titrated the dosage carefully, Cecelia knew.

Cecelia smelled the cooked meat. *That's good*, she said to herself. *Everything ought to go smoothly. Chewy will shortly be safe.* She said goodbye to her sister, packed the hamburgers balls tight into a plastic bowl, with some napkins and water, and placed them in a bag in her car. Then she grabbed her car keys.

Walking to her car, she was anxious and a little nervous, but this was exciting, like a movie. *Let's hope the tranquillisers work quickly,* she said to herself. *When we get him, she thought, we can put him in our garage – he'll be safe there until the morning.* She left by the side door and climbed into her car. Then she picked up her neighbour, Don. He had rescued dogs himself and had volunteered to help lift Chewy into Cecelia's car once the dog was knocked out. (Don also wanted to ensure Cecelia would be safe: being alone outside at night was not wise.)

Chewy didn't greet them by running along Cecelia's car that evening, but when she turned down Enslen Avenue, he was across the bridge in the park. Seeing Cecelia, he came prancing across the bridge: Cecelia's arrival meant food and attention.

'Isn't he magnificent?' Cecelia said to Don.

'He's bigger than I expected,' Don admitted.

Cecelia had parked in the middle of Enslen Avenue between the Modesto Irrigation District substation and Gary's house. With the hamburger in one hand and a leash in the other, she got out to greet Chewy.

'Here, boy,' Cecelia said. 'Isn't he lovely?'

With a slight breeze and her car doors open, Chewy knew Cecelia had food. The sweet olive oil aroma, the fragrance of cooked hamburger carried on the wind like an invisible cloud, wafted up the hill and into Chewy's moist dark long nasal cavities. He sniffed the air excitedly.

His eyes said, *Oh boy, oh boy, what have you got for me today?* Chewy danced back and forth on his hind paws but when he saw Don, his tail dropped. He backed up a tad and looked at them both. *Who was this? What's going on? Why is he here?* He stood quietly, sizing up the situation. Don stepped back a few paces.

'You go up to him, Cecelia,' he said, 'I'll back away.'

After a long pause, Chewy came slowly up to Cecelia. He let her fingers stroke his hair. A warm hot meal with wonderful smells – what more could a dog ask for? He started to eat.

Most people never watch a dog eat. Chewy was delicate, gentle and particular: he wanted his food on the ground. First, he sniffed the ground. Then he turned away as if he was not interested. He straightened up, stood back silent for a second or two, a few feet from the meatballs, then he stepped forward and lowered his head, this time directly. This time he delicately pulled his lips back, his teeth white, and gently licked the first meatball. Finally, he nibbled.

Oh no, Cecelia thought, *he smells the tranquillisers*. She tightened her lips, her checks puffing out in frustration: all that work for nothing. The wind blew her hair back away from her face. *The storm is coming*, she thought miserably. *Please eat the meatballs.*

Then he bit into one.

'Good boy, Chewy, Good boy!'

He glanced up at her, then grabbed another meat-ball between his teeth, stepped back, lifted his neck up with a tiny jerk and clamped his teeth around the meat-ball harder. Chewy swallowed and bent forward to eat another. In a few minutes all five were gone.

After eating, Chewy lay down a few feet from Cecelia at the base of the bridge. He looked at her: *That was delicious*, he seemed to say. *What's for dessert?*

Cecelia actually hadn't thought about dessert or what to do after Chewy ate the food. Being a nurse, and having seen patients tranquillised in the hospital, she thought he'd succumb relatively quickly. First, he'd get groggy, perhaps stumble a bit, and then stagger a little, fighting the effects, and finally, just laying down with his paws, forward, and his head resting comfortably between his paws. His eyes would close. He'd doze off. Maybe he'd dream with his paws and legs kicking slightly – like he was chasing a squirrel, or playing with another dog. He'd lift his head, wake up fitfully and finally roll over on his side into a deep sleep. Chewy would be knocked out by the medication in ten or fifteen minutes. Hopefully he'd just quietly go to sleep.

Ten minutes later, when Cecelia looked at Chewy, he simply stared at her blankly. He got up and stretched. *Well*, Cecelia thought. *Getting you to eat was easy. That took five minutes. We've probably got another fifteen minutes and he'll be out cold.*

'Maybe twenty minutes more?' Don suggested.

'That's what I'm hoping,' Cecelia said.

It's nice to have Don here, she thought.

They waited ten more minutes and then retreated to the car. Across the bridge the park was empty, the evening deepening into darkness before them.

Elizabeth Marshall Thomas in *The Hidden Life of Dogs* wonders what dogs experience among themselves, by themselves. What was it like to be in the mind of a dog in quiet moments? Cecelia looked at Chewy and wondered the same thing, *What's going on in his mind*?

A man in his fifties walking a Rottweiler on a leash crossed the bridge. Chewy got up to greet them. Slowed but not wobbly, Chewy sniffed them. The Rottweiler swam across the canal. Now, his haunches dripping, he stopped for Chewy to sniff. Chewy's head dropped down to smell the dog's groin. The dog stiffened, braced and jumped back. His head was up, tail alert; his body was rigid, leaning forwards on his toes.

'Cool it,' his owner said and tightened his grip on the leash, pulling the dog backwards.

That's enough for today.

'Sorry,' he yelled to Cecelia and Don.

Then the man walked away, the dog striding down the sidewalk on the other side of Cecelia's car.

'Did you see that?' said Don. 'He doesn't look drugged.'

'Not yet,' Cecilia said. Her watch said 7.30 p.m – they'd been waiting almost an hour. Chewy still looked alert – no doziness, no sluggish movements, no stumbling.

'We can't wait much longer,' Cecelia said.

Now she was worried: how long would this take? He should have been out by now.

Finally they decided to leave.

Don came back with her at 11 p.m.

Now Cecelia was really worried. She observed Chewy's breathing: he was panting. *Most likely because he was a bit anxious*, she told herself. One effect of the tranquillisers should be to slow his breathing rate but if his heart rate fell too low, especially if they'd misjudged his bodyweight, he'd be in serious trouble. She worried that they might have overdosed him. If his breathing dropped, and his heart rate lowered too much and he got very cold out here in this wind and weather by the bridge, he might die.

In the streetlight, Chewy looked alert. He still stood up. The tranquillisers should have dissolved in his stomach and passed through his intestinal walls by now, entered his bloodstream and slowed his heart rate, lowering his intake of breath until unconsciousness occurred and he collapsed back down on the asphalt. But he looked normal; he behaved normally. Were the tranquillisers not working? Had he thrown the five meatballs up?

Oh, this was getting messy. Complicated. Cecelia wished Mike was here – he'd know what to do. Or Lauren, she would help. After waiting in her car for a half-hour, Cecelia and Don realised they needed sleep and drove home.

It was one of the hardest things she'd done in this whole rescue: to leave Chewy standing in the street light by his telegraph pole, looking at her beseechingly. She backed up her car, glancing at his fading image out of her windscreen. This image haunted her as she drove home.

The empty streets cloaked in darkness reminded her just how dangerous it was. That night she had dreams of Chewy stumbling and falling and hurting himself. Of him staggering out into traffic and getting hit. Of his breathing falling so low, he died. Died alone. Cecelia woke up suddenly, her first thought, 'Chewy!' It was 4 a.m., she could not wait for daylight. Chewy had been out in the night with tranquillisers in him, she had to get back to the canal, now. She couldn't wait for a decent hour to ask Don or Charlotte to come with her: she would go back alone; it would be fine.

Cecelia dressed in silence and drove through the calm streets past bus stops, shuttered houses, a skateboard and three bikes still locked to the back of a station wagon carrier. She scanned the two sides of the street, holding her head over the steering wheel, hoping to find Chewy safe when she turned onto Enslen Avenue and drove towards the substation. After so little sleep, she was worried: surely he's knocked out by now?

Cool air blew in as she drove. *Oh, he's OK. My special boy*, she thought. *Let him be OK*. She parked her car, stepped out and walked towards Gary's house. Chewy wasn't lying in the grass; he wasn't at his telegraph pole.

She checked the bushes by the substation: nothing, not even a hair. *He's got to be behind the bushes beside Gary's house, at least I hope he is*, she thought. It was hard to see in the bushes in the dark. She crouched down at the end of the bushes for a look along the fence. In the dark she couldn't see. *Is he lying along the fence?* Cecelia frowned. She walked up the cement sidewalk to the small slab that was Gary's front porch. The house was dark, inside everyone was sleeping: Gary, his daughter, her boyfriend and their young child.

What if they saw her, a strange shadow poking around outside their front door? What if they called the cops? Or Gary came out with his shotgun?

This was not a smart position to be in. Cecelia paused for a moment – *What am I going to do?* She turned around, facing right and looking down the street.

Just then she noticed him: Chewy's legs were sticking out from under Gary's parked car in the carport. His body was hidden by the car. *Good for you*, Cecelia thought, *Good for you, my little Chewy! You took care of yourself. Now, what am I going I do?*

She decided she'd have to drag him to the car. The street was still dark; Gary's house was dark. Standing in the carport, she whispered softly to a passed-out Chewy, 'My little Chewy, I'm going to pull you out here across the grass to my car. You're safe, honey. Just let me get a hold of your legs.' Cecelia bent down and tried to slide her arms under Chewy's front legs.

She worried again about waking everyone in the house, thinking someone would shoot her, or Chewy. *Probably me*, she thought to herself.

She felt something bump against her leg. A cold chill came over her. *Oh no*, she thought.

She waited for a commanding voice in the darkness to tell her to freeze, to not move. When she looked down, it was Ginger, bumping her muzzle against her thigh, curious.

'Ginger, Ginger,' she whispered, 'you scared me to death!' Ginger walked over to Chewy, sniffed him and then came back to Cecelia. Cecelia had the loop leash around her neck as she bent forwards on her hands and knees to look at Chewy under Gary's car.

Ginger bumped Cecelia in her butt, then she nudged Chewy. On all fours, Cecelia told herself to be calm: *Ginger is just trying to help to keep things calm.* She sat up. In the carport beside Gary's parked car she saw a bedroom window. Someone in Gary's household was probably sound asleep just on the other side. *OK*, she thought, *if at first you don't succeed, try and try again.*

She got down on her knees, tucked Chewy's tail in between his legs and put her hands on his hindquarters and pushed. His rump was still warm, his fur made it hard to feel for his hip bones. She strained, leaned forwards, put her full weight into pushing his rump but Chewy didn't move. He didn't slide down the cement – it was like two pieces of cement scratching against each other.

Then Ginger nudged Chewy again.

Chewy raised his head up and looked over his shoulder at Ginger as if he might wake up. Then his head bent back down into his chest.

'Shush,' Cecelia told Ginger. 'Don't bark. Be quiet! We don't want to wake Gary, or anybody else.'

Ginger nudged Chewy. He moved. Cecelia bent back down to see Chewy's full body and tried to get her hands under his front legs to move him.

Ginger nudged Chewy again. This time she circled around behind Cecelia and nudged Chewy's dark body on the buttocks.

Cecelia whispered to Ginger, 'Thank you, Ginger, we're in here trying to help Chewy, aren't we, Ginger? You're such a good girl.'

Suddenly Chewy's head lifted. His legs kicked and scrambled. He struggled to get himself to his feet, scampering in slow motion, and clumsily crawled out from under Gary's car. Now he was up on his own four feet, wobbly and looking dazed. Then he fell. Groggily, he sat up. He sat motionless for a few seconds trying to figure out what was going on and why he felt so sleepy.

Cecelia put her hands on either side of Chewy to steady him. Chewy twisted free and turned to scamper off but only succeeded in scraping his paws against the cement, going nowhere. He wanted to walk down the side of the car and go round to the front wing.

Cecelia danced around in front of him and directed him away from the carport. Chewy fell against Cecelia's body. She tried to steady him and put her hands under his front legs to move him forwards but she couldn't. Then she remembered the leash: *I'd better get that on him so he can't run away*, she thought. She tried, but Chewy was fighting her, turning his head right and left to avoid the loop leash. Even groggy, he knew what a leash meant.

Then Ginger came alongside Chewy and nudged him: he wouldn't budge. She nudged him again. Cecelia smiled to herself – 'Good girl, Ginger.' *Thank God for Ginger*! 'But I've got to get a leash on him, Ginger – he might wake up fully and be gone before I can stop him.'

Quickly, Cecelia called Chewy's name. Groggily, he looked up. Then she reached over Chewy's shoulder and slipped the leash over his head. She pulled the leash back along his body with one hand and nudged him forwards with the other. His head and skin moved like rubbery elastic when she pulled on them. When Chewy tried to turn, she restrained him with her forearm and the leash. His head lifting and his shoulders rising, he staggered forwards on his own. He then slouched back down.

This is crazy, Cecelia thought, *I should have asked Don to come with me. He could lift him*. She sat down next to Chewy in the semi-dark carport. *What am I going to do?*

If anyone happens to drive or walk by now how am I going to explain the fact that I'm a sixty-five-year-old woman, trying to drag a drugged dog down Gary's driveway at 4.30 a.m.? Would they believe me? Would I believe myself? What if someone calls the cops? I hope they do. If the police came, I'd get them to help me. She thought for a moment. *Maybe not – after all, I'm in jeans, and a sweatshirt – all dark colours, colours a thief might wear. My hair is messed up, my car door is open... Did I bring my wallet? My driver's licence?*

She could just hear the police talking between themselves. 'Think she's on drugs?' 'Listen,' the older policeman would say, 'What do you do, lady? A nurse, really? Oh yeah? Of course you're a registered nurse. A sixty-five-year-old registered nurse who drugged a stray dog with prescription tranquillisers but she doesn't know their name or the dosages she used. She's wandering around in a strange neighbourhood, not her own, in the dark at 4.30 in the morning.

'She's in front of a house whose owner's last name she doesn't know and she claims she's trying to drag a passed-out dog across the wet grass to her car so she can take it to a vet whose office is conveniently closed and she doesn't know when the clinic opens. How do we know you're not stealing the dog? How do we know this isn't a vendetta against the guy you claim lives here? Do you want us to wake them up? Listen lady, if you're a registered nurse, then I'm King Kong and Modesto is Jurassic Park.'

Yep, Cecelia thought. *I'd better whisper and be quick.* She danced around Chewy again, trying to pull him forwards.

Chewy kept struggling to get free. Cecelia kept the leash tight around his neck and along his body just in case he stood up and tried to get away. Lifting him was impossible. She tried to encourage him forwards. No way, her back couldn't take it. She tried the great compression technique, where she put her arms under and behind his rear legs and under and around his chest, squeezed and hoped to lift him forwards in small scoops. *Dream on*, she said to herself, *I can't budge him*.

Instead she let Ginger and Chewy stumble forwards in their own way and in their own time. She merely helped by some prodding and by letting Chewy lean up against her legs when he looked like he'd fall or needed to stop for a rest. It was slow going.

Finally, after much effort, they made it to Cecelia's car. Next to her car, Cecelia sat down, tired, on Gary's grass. She looked out across the street: Michele's house was dark. The night was beautiful, except she had an eighty-pound, passed-out dog in her lap. Cecelia rubbed Chewy's head and muzzle. She bent over and kissed him on the forehead. 'I'm sorry,' she said. 'I'm sorry to have to put you through this.'

She checked the loop leash: Chewy was still leashed securely. He continued to move slowly, his eyes a little glassy; his breathing was regular if not a little slow. His body was relaxed but still stubbornly resistant to moving. *Thank God*, Cecelia thought, *Ginger's been a big help! Ginger kept things calm*. At the car, Chewy stood parallel to the car, head towards the engine and rump facing the boot.

OK, Cecelia said to herself, *I got him this far now, how do I lift him into the car?*

Again, she bent over, pushing her arms under Chewy's body. With the car door open as she'd left it, she cleared paper and a small box off the seat before taking a blanket she had from the front seat. She laid it across the curved back seat as a cushion, rolled the window down and knelt back over Chewy. He was standing silently, eyes closed, a bit wobbly; the leash was dangling around his neck between his feet.

With her arms under Chewy's hindquarters and front shoulders, Cecelia tried to lift Chewy into the back seat. She got him up onto her left knee and tried to push him closer to the back seat: he was heavy, way too heavy. She couldn't lift him further up into the seat in one swoop. Cecelia spun sideways and tried to slip him onto the seat as if he was a giant sausage. She got his head and shoulders on the seat but nothing more. Stuck there for a moment, she wondered what to do: Chewy's head and shoulders lay on the seat, his rear and hindquarters dangling out the back door. Slowly, like a limp rag, he slipped back onto the asphalt. Then he raised his head and struggled again to lift himself.

'Oh, my poor Chewy,' Cecelia whispered. 'Oh honey, lay quiet – this will be over soon. Don't hurt yourself. I'm sorry, I'm *so* sorry.'

His head collapsed back down.

This was hard, Cecelia thought, *but at least I'm making some progress.* She looked at the flattened grass Chewy had struggled across and could see the path in the grass. *If I can just lift him into the car, everything will be all right*, she thought. But he was too heavy.

Surprisingly, Chewy did not utter a sound. No barking. Just his silent breath as Cecelia thought about what to do next. Her arms ached, she felt herself drifting off; the heaviness in her body. *When it gets tough, the tough get going. I can do this*, she told herself. She nudged herself back awake: nothing was going to stop her now. *It's going to be a long, long day but in the end Chewy will be off the street and safe. My little Chewy will have a home!*

Cecelia hoped no cars would come down the street. Their headlights might catch her and Chewy crumpled on the street. She'd look like a frightened deer. Already she could see her picture in the morning paper: Woman caught stealing neighbour's dog. She'd be embarrassed. *OK*, she said to herself. *I got him this far, now how do I lift him into the car?*

Determined, Cecelia tried again, *God, he is heavy*, she said to herself.

This is hopeless, I can't lift him, she thought. *What am I going to do?* Cecelia leaned against the rear side panel of her car. *Well, I'll just have to wait till someone comes along*, she decided. Ten minutes went by. Another five and then she heard two women talking. Cecelia stood up. Two women were just walking over the canal bridge and talking. In tennis shoes, slacks and pullover jackets, they were getting their morning exercise before work.

As they walked by Cecelia's car one of them said, 'We didn't see you there.'

'Oh yes,' Cecelia said, 'I'm here!' Her eyes were on Chewy. Cecelia had taken her blue sweatshirt off and laid it over Chewy's body. If his temperature got too low, he might stop breathing. She knew CPR – she'd just breathe into his nose and massage his chest if she had to. *This dog is going to make it*!

She looked at the women. Cecelia thought about just how she would ask for help. Before she could do so, the women had walked around her car and saw Chewy fast asleep in the street with a sweatshirt over him. He looked like a lumpy sack of potatoes.

'Oh,' one of the women said. She saw the blue sweatshirt over Chewy's body. 'How touching,' she added.

'Is that a dead dog?' asked the other woman.

'No,' Cecelia said. She explained everything.

'He looks heavy…' the first woman questioned.

'But kind of peaceful,' the other woman said. She smiled at Cecelia as she bent her head around sideways to look at Chewy's face. 'Oh,' she said, 'this is the dog by the bridge.'

As they were discussing their options, one of the women noticed the paper man coming down the street.

'I know this guy – he delivers our papers. He's great, he'll help us,' she said.

The smaller woman walked out into the middle of the street, waving her arms. An older blue car came down the street. Rich Antal and his wife delivered newspapers early, usually before 5 a.m. so people had their papers with their morning coffee. He was pitching papers out the left driver's side window while driving. His wife rolled the newspapers in the back seat of the car; she threw the right side of the street. They threw almost 350 papers a day with a total of three different paper routes. Working as an effective team, the route took about two hours plus the time it took to fold and pick up the newspapers.

Rich Antal had had this route for almost ten years. He'd seen some surreal things early in the morning in Modesto delivering papers. At first, he didn't see the three women. He was leaning out his driver's side window, throwing a paper towards his customer's porch. Just as he turned his head to pull himself back in the car to get the next paper, his wife said, 'Rich, what is that?'

He leaned out his car window – 'Need any help, ladies?'

When he got out of his car to help, he recognised the two women walkers as his customers. He also recognised Cecelia as another customer. He then saw Chewy lying in the street

'Can you lift him?' Cecelia asked.

'Does he bite?' he responded.

She told him Chewy's story. As Rich listened, he thought, *I've seen this dog on the streets when I'm delivering papers. That's the dog that was over by the oleander bushes on Virginia Avenue before the trail was built. Yeah, he's the one I tried to rescue.* He was about to ask Cecelia how she got him, when Cecelia said, 'Tranquillisers. We tranquillised him, that's why he's passed out. Can you help lift him onto the back seat of my car?'

At five foot ten and 190 pounds, Rich still had the strength from his college track and field days. Coaching at a local high school track kept him in shape. When he bent over Chewy, he laid the leash down. His wife got out of the car and helped. Rich lifted Chewy's shoulders and head and his wife lifted Chewy's back legs and flanks. In one slow, careful movement they lifted and gently laid Chewy on Cecelia's back car seat. Chewy's front legs stuck out awkwardly, his back legs hung out the door. Rich gently shoved Chewy's feet to the left so he could push the back door shut. As he did so, he pushed the door lock down with his left hand.

'There,' he said, 'Safe and sound.'

'Good job,' the smaller woman said, smiling at Rich. 'You deserve a special doggie angel award.'

Then Rich and his wife drove off.

'Thank God, I've got you, Chewy!' Cecelia said.

Chewy was off the streets and safe!

Chapter Ten
In the Hospital

I lay naked on the gurney, under the rough knotted thermal sheet the hospital put over me.

The doctor said, 'Mr Klein – Bruce isn't it? – can you hear me clearly?'

Raising my head, I could see Lauren next to the doctor, who was talking from behind clear glass into a microphone. The room was empty, cold and filled with a giant-screen TV. To my left was a grey slab of a body scanner retracted back up closer to the ceiling. The institutional grey walls were depressing and I was scared.

'Mr Klein,' the doctor said, 'Please look to your left at the monitor.'

I turned my head and focused on the screen, which was buzzing white static. At first, I thought my vision was affected by the medication they'd given me, then the screen cleared and a series of thin black wiggly lines appeared against the white static that clarified into a simple screen with a white background. The lines were very black and I could see them clearly now.

'Those are your heart vessels,' the doctor said. 'See the one where the cursor is, that's the one that's blocked 80 per cent, your left descending artery that goes down the left side of your heart.

'It's the one that has been giving you trouble. You've given us permission to put stents in, and I will do that now. Please try not to move and breathe regularly.'

Breathe regularly, I thought, *what planet is this guy from? I'm sedated, flat on my back, depressed, naked and scared. My wife is frightened behind that screen and I'm thinking if this doctor hiccups, I'm dead for sure. Sure I'll be still, I got no complaints. Without you guys, I'd be dead. So what's the alternative?*

The alternative they'd explained to me last night.

* * *

Last night, the head doctor for that shift said, 'If you don't allow us to insert stents tomorrow, we'll have to discharge you against medical advice and you'll go to the end of the line.'

Great, I'd thought. I'd come in with a small chest tightness and now I had to make a life-and-death decision under duress. Important medical decisions I really didn't know anything about. *My wife isn't here. I don't know diddly squat about this stenting procedure – whether it's necessary, or if there are other options like medication available elsewhere.* The whole thing felt rushed and I wanted out; I wanted time to research my options.

'How can I make a decision without a second opinion, without gathering some information, without talking to my primary care doctor?' I asked.

Lauren was not with me while I was in the emergency room. She was still recovering from her major surgery; only two weeks into recovery. During that time my left arm had occasionally felt like a stuffed sausage but I'd dismissed it. Then one afternoon, locking my studio door, my left hand started tingling and my left arm began throbbing. Again, I dismissed it. When I sat down at my computer inside the house, tightness in my chest scared me. Something was wrong, I told myself.

I mentioned to Lauren that I was going to see my doctor. I had left the house thinking I would be home in an hour. When I was told to go straight to the ER, I called Lauren and told her what was happening. She still could not drive and volunteered to have her mother drop her off at the emergency room. Since she was still vulnerable to infection I told her to stay at home although I wished she was here to help me decipher what was happening. I decided I would call her.

The doctor smiled at me. I wondered where he'd learned his bedside manner – he needed to take a remedial course. When I looked at him I thought to myself, *He must think I'm a difficult patient because I am asking all of these questions. He will discharge me against medical advice if I don't do what he wants.* I knew what that meant in terms of my medical insurance – likely exclusion. What if I didn't do this stenting procedure: could I line up a second opinion fast enough before I had a heart attack? How likely was that? Were there even any other treatments? Who could I go to for advice? A mistake here could be fatal, and I had no idea how probable that was.

I stopped myself from this negative thinking, reminding myself that he was not the enemy. *He's trying to help you, to save your life, you dumb ass*, my internal dialogue continued. *You did this to yourself – all that junk food, all those years.*

'Can I think about it overnight?' I asked.

The doctor smiled, empathy clearly expressed on his face. 'Sure,' he said, 'just let us know after you and your wife have made a decision.'

He took my hand as a reassuring gesture, held it for a moment and then quickly left the room. I felt confused, angry and afraid. What did they know? Then I remembered I was medicated out of my mind.

* * *

To cut a long story short, I had three stents inserted in the one damaged artery. I was deeply thankful.

I'd dodged two bullets, prostate cancer and now a heart attack, a year apart from each other. Two major causes of death for older men. The road back wasn't easy, I was just glad to be alive now.

Chapter Eleven
Off the Streets

Tears slowly ran down Cecelia's cheeks. She made little whimpering sounds; she didn't burst out into a full-throated sobs. No one heard her moan or even noticed her tears. Slightly embarrassed, she quickly wiped the tears away with the back of her hand and stood back along the front wing of her car.

Two vet technicians from Maze Animal Hospital walked towards the vehicle. They rolled a cart to carry Chewy from Cecelia's car back inside of the clinic. Bouncing over black asphalt, the cart jiggled. Suddenly, Mike came out of the clinic, walking towards the car.

'All right, where is this dog?' he quipped.

Mike worked hard to make his clinic the best veterinarian clinic in Modesto. Kind, devoted to animals, he held strong opinions about most topics related to animals. He'd worked long hours during the summer earning money for vet school and had driven himself tirelessly to save animals: big or small, cats or dogs, cattle or wild creatures.

Cecelia was relieved to see him.

In the shadow of his clinic, he bent over and looked cautiously in the back seat of Cecelia's car. Cecelia's eyes slowly followed Mike's arms as they slid under the groggy body of Chewy, his left hand cradling the dog's head. He lifted Chewy out of the car and turned in one great slow arch, settling him in his arms. Then he walked to his clinic. It was all over in less than two minutes. The two vet technicians smiled knowingly to each other as one opened the clinic door. 'Hey, Mike,' said one, grinning, 'need any help?'

'Nah,' Mike smiled, bending down and turning sideways as he slipped through the door. 'I got it covered.'

It was typical Mike behaviour – what's the big deal? Let's just get the job done!

Watching Mike and Chewy disappear, Cecelia closed her eyes. *Oh, my lovely Chewy*, she thought, *you're safe now*. Relieved and surprised by her own sadness, she sighed: *Now, what? I guess that's over with. I can go to work now*. She turned to go. A shimmered reflection off the glass door of the clinic startled her as Mike's head popped out the door.

'Have you got a minute?' he asked Cecelia. 'We need some particulars.'

Check-in required information: rescue details, costs, phone numbers, names and addresses, and facts about Chewy. While Cecelia answered these questions and filled out paperwork, down the hall in another room Mike examined Chewy.

A drugged Chewy lay calmly on the exam table, his head bent in and tucked against the stainless steel rim of the table. Mike inserted a thermometer, and waited: Chewy's temperature was normal. His hands followed the gentle slope of Chewy's shoulders, feeling for tender spots. They paused for a moment. His right hand placed his stethoscope off-centre under Chewy's right shoulder. The slow, constant two beats, lub-dub, evenly spaced and strong, told Mike how the blood flowed in Chewy's body. Then Mike began checking Chewy's eyes, ears and teeth. He stroked Chewy's fur up and down, looking for fleas, checking the texture of Chewy's fur, the thick or thinness of his skin.

Moderately surprised, Mike thought, *Chewy has no major problems*. He passed his hand down the thigh, traced the curve of the hock and held each paw clasped in his closed hand for a second, in a small blessing. Looking down at the limp body before him Mike thought, *How magnificent, how brilliant, this mystery of life is*.

Chewy, breathing shallowly, lay quietly on the exam table. Mike watched his chest fur rise and fall.

Nothing, he told himself, *nothing of clinical significance. A slight sore spot, a tender area here and there, but overall Chewy appears surprisingly healthy*. It was a minor miracle for a dog who had lived on the street for a year and a half.

Lauren will be happy, Mike said to himself. *He's one lucky dog – in good health and nothing seriously wrong with him. No injuries. No scars from dog fights. No cracked teeth, and all these people caring about him. One lucky dog!*

During Chewy's exam, Cecelia finished the paperwork and then drove to work.

* * *

Earlier that morning, at 6.15 a.m. she had called Lauren.

'Lauren,' she said, 'I'm worried.'

The fear in Cecelia's voice woke Lauren. On painkillers, she slept soundly, not worrying a lot about Chewy. But hearing Cecelia's voice worried her.

'He didn't stumble in traffic, did he?'

'No, no,' responded Cecelia.

'He's OK, isn't he?'

'He's at my house. He's snoring in the back seat of my car, parked just outside my house, passed out but his breathing is so slow and shallow, I'm worried. What time does Mike's clinic open?'

'7a.m.'

'Thank goodness,' Cecelia said. 'Charlotte can watch him close, while I get ready for work. I'll call you later with more news after I drop him off at Mike's.'

At 11a.m., Cecelia called Lauren back and told her what had happened overnight when rescuing Chewy, before adding, 'Chewy is safe with Mike now.'

'Cecelia, I can't believe it – you got Chewy off the streets!' Lauren said. 'I'm so happy. After all our efforts we can relax a bit, knowing he is off the street and safe.'

You've done a good thing, Cecelia thought to herself. An hour later, while working, she was lost in the routine of a nurse's day. She was tired but relieved because Chewy was finally safe and sound.

* * *

In bed, two hours later, Lauren called Mike for an update on Chewy. She knows he's busy, she knows he'll call back – but when would Mike call her back? She wanted those details. How could she sleep? How could *anyone* sleep? Waiting drove her nuts. Was he OK? Did he have parasites from living on the street? How long would he be drugged out, wobbly and staggering around? Could he hurt himself at Mike's? Would he fight them? Cause trouble? Would they be able to clean him up? Would he let them get close? What if he had injuries, or was malnourished? How long did he need to be at Mike's and at what expense? Did Mike do blood work on Chewy and if so, what had it revealed? Any organs harmed from street food? A lot could have gone wrong, especially since he had lived on the streets since a puppy. Lauren had a thousand questions, she needed a thousand answers, now.

Finally, she fell asleep. That evening she got her update. When Mike said there was nothing significantly wrong with Chewy, it was such a relief. Lauren lay back in her bed, resting. What a gift! He was safe and relatively healthy. What would be the next step, she wondered. She asked Mike over the phone.

'Oh, the usual routine,' Mike said. 'I've already examined him and started him on the shots he needs. Tomorrow, I'll neuter him. He will have a couple of days of drugs in him – between tranquillising him and neutering him. We will watch him closely. He weighs around sixty pounds so we'll work on getting some weight on him. He should probably weigh closer to seventy-five pounds for his size and age.'

Lauren, surprised, wondered why. Everyone in the neighbourhood was leaving Chewy food; he had plenty of food available. *Maybe he's a finicky eater. His thick fur must have hidden how underweight he was. Maybe street life is tougher than I thought?*

Lauren knew Chewy needed shots and neutering. Bruce was against neutering. She figured it was a male thing – gonad to gonad, so to speak. He had no problem spaying Emma.

She pulled the comforter around herself and closed her eyes. Now she could sleep, and she did. When she woke, she had one more question.

What was next for Chewy?

When she woke she also had the answer: THE PLAN.

Chewy would be neutered, he'd get an ID chip and then it was off to Top Notch Kennels for two weeks and finally, to our neighbours, Denise and Rob, for two weeks. That would give her almost six weeks of healing. Her sore stomach would be healed by then, for sure. Healed, she would then have two weeks with

Chewy to adjust to his new home before she had to go back to work.

Thank heaven for Denise, Lauren thought. Without Denise and Rob's help, the plan would be much more difficult. Rob and Denise lived behind and around the corner from us. We shared an alleyway with them and we'd discovered they were also dog lovers. While talking about rescuing Chewy, Denise mentioned their dog Boss, a Rottweiler mix, had played with Chewy in the park. Chewy liked Boss.

When Denise realised Cecelia had drugged Chewy, that the rescue was half completed, and Lauren could not take care of him until she was healed, Denise agreed to house Chewy for two weeks. That gave Lauren enough time to heal completely. Denise's generosity stunned me.

* * *

When Chewy woke at the clinic, he woke slowly, groggily, stumbling to stand on his four paws. Scraping his claws against the stainless steel floor at the back of his kennel, he fought to stand up. His eyes struggled to focus. As the last of his drowsiness and confusion fell away, his breathing increased and his heart rate returned to normal.

What are these smells?

Fear and anxiety came back into his pupils, constricting under bright lights. He stared out, blankly and quietly. All these smells were new. Trace smells of urine surrounded him. Scents of perfume from female vet techs washed over him. The antibacterial smell of cleaning agents used to wash down floors and cages, Rocal–d plus, alcohol scents, pheromones of strange new dogs telling histories of travels, sexual readiness, age and health issues lingered on the floors and doors. He smelt the gentle new hands of other human handlers as they carried other dogs back and forth before his cage. In the first few hours a rich new mysterious and puzzling new symphony of smells swirled around, floated into and down Chewy's nasal passages. His brain struggled to decipher, decode and make sense of them.

Dark blue jeans walking past the bars of his kennel taught him as much as the yelping and barking in the background. Doors were opening and creaking shut. Country music played in the background, with lights going on and off as vet techs disinfected the thickly painted cement floor. The mop head squishing across the floor, leaving a trail of white bubbles. Above him to his right was an intercom with a twanging guitar in the background. These strange noises and new smells clogged Chewy's brain.

If he were human, Chewy would be bewildered and confused; frightened and anxious. A stranger in a foreign land where he didn't understand the native tongue, couldn't read the visual clues he saw, or understand the signs. These people weren't like those he saw in the park, or near the canal bridge. Their odours were new and different – a pungent, sweet and acidic brew impossible to decipher entirely.

What's happening? Chewy wondered. *Where am I? What's going on?* Chewy's street smarts became his defence. *Best to lie low and observe, wait for a chance to escape.*

At first he refused food. The sick smells of other ill animals bothered him – he knew what those smells meant, it was in his DNA. The sickness was on the hands of those who brought him food. Wary, he backed himself up against the rear of his cage as far as he could get from those hands and their odour. But the hands reached in with their antiseptic scent and leashed him, then walked him through the clinic's rooms, rich with new aromas to the back door.

When he stepped into sunlight, he smelled pine needles, the fragrance of dried leaves, dog poop and garbage behind the buildings, parked cars and worn tyres. Excited, he sniffed along the fence. He understood these smells.

These were familiar smells he knew from the park and the canal – wooden benches, maple and oak trees, puddles of dirty water, dog spray and markings on telegraph poles. All these odours flooded his nasal cavities but a seven-foot fence with a tarpaulin over it blocked his view. He could hear engines racing, children yelling, someone cutting grass. In the distance a truck with its brakes screeched to a halt. One moment the smells of mystery, the next the old smells of freedom.

Two or three times a day a vet assistant took him on these brief walks. Always on a leash, always these familiar sounds and smells reassured him and yet at the same time they confused him. Chewy wanted to get out, to get back to the canal, to what he knew. He was trapped in a big change that he didn't understand. What would come next?

After a few days Lauren and I went to see Chewy. Although we knew Mike would take great care of him, we needed to see him for ourselves. We needed to see how he was coping. Chewy was kept in a stainless steel cage in one of the rooms in the back of the clinic. While the cage was large, it was not a place to leave a large dog for long but as Chewy was still recuperating from the drugs, the shots and the surgery, Lauren felt he was all right for now. He would shortly be on his way to Top Notch Kennels, where there would be more room for him.

* * *

Chewy did what survival on the streets had taught him to do: lay low, try to hide and become watchful. Not hostile, nor agitated or aggressive, but watchful and waiting. Waiting for a chance to escape. Always, there was a way to escape. No wonder he was tentative, cautious and skittish. He looked for his escape opportunity. At Mike's vet clinic, he never found one.

* * *

After Mike's, Denise drove Lauren and Chewy in her new Prius five miles north to Top Notch Kennels. Chewy had never been in a car or on a freeway before. Panicked, he paced back and forth, panting the entire drive. At Top Notch, Denise drove into a gated parking area. If Chewy escaped, he would be safe in a parking area and not running loose in the streets.

Top Notch wasn't Chewy's escape opportunity either. Like the vet clinic it was escape-proof. Both establishments were staffed by caring, loving people, who treated dogs impeccably. To a street-wise dog, bred on and used to freedom, quality of care didn't matter, though. It didn't particularly because Chewy was young and full of adolescent energy; he wanted out. He thrived on excitement, adventure and curiosity. Chewy wanted out now, to what he knew, to the familiar.

Not that he was ever rude.

At Top Notch they give the owner of each animal they take care of a report card on six dimensions of the animal's behaviour while boarding with them. Chewy's report card grading his stay gave him straight As in every category bar eating. That was the funny thing with Chewy – his not eating. You would think since he was on the streets, he would chow down everything placed in front of him. Not Chewy. He was rather particular about food, allowing stress to derail his eating.

While at Top Notch, Chewy was evaluated on how social he was with dogs. Dog play is Chewy's speciality, group play his love. In doggie playgroups, dogs put together by temperament, age and compatibility are let loose in a large fenced play yard. In group play he passed with flying colours – after all, other dogs were Chewy's first companions, it was people who made him nervous.

So Chewy had plenty of playtime at Top Notch; daily play groups, sniffing and smelling during normal kennel routines. Lauren paid extra for the kennel staff to walk and talk with Chewy, one on one. Soothing tones and gentle hands softened his skittish fear. This socialisation was a beginning.

During the two weeks Chewy was in Top Notch, Denise first, and then Lauren's mother Barbara, drove Lauren out to visit Chewy to see how he was doing and to spend time with him. At home, Lauren wondered how he'd healed from surgery. Was he happy? Really eating? What did he look like groomed? Glowing reports couldn't match her eyeballing him. At the kennel she could see how he was doing and spend time with him. She hadn't healed enough to drive so Denise and her mom chauffeured her back and forth from Top Notch.

A wonderful neighbour and a dutiful mom, Lauren felt blessed.

During these visits, Lauren sat with Chewy near the front desk. The reception area swarmed with dogs, all pushing and shoving. Little dogs were being dropped off, big dogs suddenly appeared from around corners; other dogs were swirling out of sight. Always there were two or three dogs at the front desk sniffing, barking, play bumping or straining on leashes. Some dogs just sat quietly at their master's feet. The kennel floor was a sea of snouts, upturned eyes, tongues licking and tails everywhere swishing. This bustling activity would keep any dog excited, especially Chewy – he loved it. He pulled at his leash, sniffing and rough housing. Each new dog visitor was a wild new adventure more interesting than Lauren.

On one such visit, Tom and his wife Dee, also friends and neighbours, came to see Chewy. Dee has a particular fondness for Boxers and they had two of their own. Chewy had become good friends with Jake and Nevada while living on the streets. Tom walked their dogs in our neighbourhood or along the canal. He'd fed Chewy and both he and Dee had tried to get him off the streets. On that particular visit to Top Notch they had come specifically to see Chewy: it was a nice, caring touch.

Chapter Twelve
The First Escape

After two weeks at the kennels, the transition to Denise's house was easy. Denise drove Lauren to Top Notch in her Prius one last time to pick up Chewy. Then they drove home to Denise's house. When he was put into the back seat of the Prius, Denise left the back seat window slightly open. The wind blew in a bouquet of scents Chewy had almost forgotten: cow manure as they drove home through the rich farmland along Highway 99, a swirl of gaseous odours – hot engine oils and exhaust fumes, and bits of dirt as trucks swarmed by – and then turning down the tree-lined streets near Graceada Park: the dry, crumbly scent of rushed oak leaves rotting in gutters and dead straw-coloured grasses piled along the street kerb.

Chewy was leashed in a security harness but still bounced around, wide-eyed and curious. What's this new place? Chewy knew these smells.

Going down the alleyway to the garage at Denise's house, Chewy smelled garbage stench, heard barking dogs and saw a big white cat. The cat walked along the six-foot redwood fence opposite the garage entrance and stopped when the Prius stopped.

When Lauren pushed the door of the silver Prius open inside the garage she felt pain. *Almost four weeks since the surgery, four whole weeks!* she thought. How long was this going to take? She pivoted on the seat, her right and then her left leg swung out the door onto the cement of Denise's garage.

When she stood up, she experienced still more pain in her abdomen. *Oh, all right, we'll call it a draw*, she thought, smiling to herself as she thought of Monty Python's Black Knight ''Tis but a scratch' sketch.

'Are you all right?' Denise asked.

Denise had driven directly into her garage so Chewy had no chance to escape. During the weekdays her husband Rob's car was gone while he was working and she had thought it would be easier to bring Chewy home when there was only one car in the garage. Denise popped open the rear door to unload Chewy and his stuff into the empty garage.

'I need to go rest,' Lauren said. 'I'm sorry I can't help but thank you so much for everything.'

Lauren was exhausted.

But Chewy was excited. He smelled Boss in this car; he smelled Boss in the garage. When he was put in the back seat of the Prius to drive home, an ocean of new air currents suddenly filled his moist, shiny black nostrils: perfumes on the bodies of the two women who visited him, their car reeking of a dog's smell he knew, a dog he played with, and then those street smells again. Chewy pressed his nose against the back window: what was going on? His head turned curiously, eyes wide open, looking out eagerly.

In a short fifteen minutes Chewy's stuff was unloaded. He was inside Denise's backyard, greeting Boss. Elated and happy, he was nipping and tucking, his chest bumping; relieved.

Chewy explored the new backyard, sniffing along the fence. *Not much opportunity to escape here*, Denise thought as she watched him from her back porch.

She and Rob had checked the fence just in case. *You're our guest for two weeks, Chewy*, she thought. *Might as well make the best of it.* Boss came up beside Chewy, nipping at his left front leg in an invitation to play.

In the next two days Chewy settled in quickly, except for eating. He sniffed his food, but left it uneaten. No problem for Boss, who ate all the extra food.

One day, Denise was looking out her kitchen window when she saw Boss but no Chewy. The backyard looked empty. *Maybe*, she thought, *he's hiding in the dark shadows or the corner bushes?* Chewy was flattened against the ground surveying his new domain, his nostrils sniffing the scents as Denise's legs walked by. He saw her hand set his bowl of raw food down on the grass.

It takes time, Denise told herself as she looked around. *He's not in the shadow of the garage; he's not in the bushes, or by the corner. Perhaps he's along the side of the house up front by the gate, hoping to escape? He's a sweetie but you can't be careless with him.* She walked back into her house, smiling to herself.

Raw food must be a new diet for him, she told herself. *Well, what a lucky dog – he's getting carrots, corn, elk, some chicken breasts. What's not to like? Raw food, it's the healthiest way to go! I should eat so good myself,* she thought. *It's only been two days since he last ate, he'll come out of his secret hiding place and eat today.*

Boss certainly did. She could hear his guttural munching as she watched him devouring his food, head bent over, buried in his food bowl. Now older, he had slowed down – but not his eating. Denise had without hesitation volunteered to caretake Chewy while Lauren healed. Having Boss and Chewy together for two weeks gave Boss a play pal – it was like a play date, only for dogs. *But where is Chewy?* she wondered. Denise stepped back into the kitchen.

When she checked for Chewy a few minutes later, Boss and Chewy were eating together only a few feet from her in the backyard. Chewy's eyes widened when he looked up at her, brown chicken sauce dripping from his jaws. He paused for a second, snorted and then his tongue licked his lips. Then his head bent down into the raw food. *I've been waiting for this,* he seemed to be saying, *I love chicken breasts.*

Took you long enough, Denise thought, *but I knew you'd love it. You're an interesting dog, Chewy.*

What a treat to watch Boss and Chewy playing together, Denise thought. She had tried to rescue Chewy herself several times before Lauren and Cecelia rescued him. During her rescue attempts she thought if he smelt treats, he'd come up to her. With a little luck, she could slip a collar around him.

Sure enough, at the canal bridge he'd smelt treats and come up, but Chewy was smart: he never got close enough for her to slip a collar on him. Always he stayed just out of reach. On one knee leaning forwards she'd hold the treats out in her left hand. He'd be barely out of reach. When she reached forwards to collar him, she'd be off balance and briefly lurch forwards, which gave him just enough time to jerk back.

Just enough time to avoid a leash, a collar and to escape.

Oh, he was a smart one, that Chewy!

Dozens of others in the neighbourhood had tried to slip a collar on Chewy but they had all failed. In the year and a half before Lauren and Cecelia decided to drug him, who knew how many had tried and failed to rescue him? He was somewhat of a minor urban legend near Graceada Park – the hobo dog everyone worried about. A ghost dog that appeared and then disappeared.

He even followed Boss and myself home, twice, Denise thought to herself, recalling each adventure.

Each time Chewy looked like he wanted to come in, particularly since Boss was there, but then he would not go through the front door or side gate. He'd play with Boss in the park and follow him to Denise's house. Denise remembered they were so joyous together.

'I thought this could be perfect. If I open the gate, Chewy would follow Boss into our backyard,' Denise told me. 'So I unlocked the gate and pushed it open. Boss went prancing in. I was excited but Chewy just sat down before the gate, looking in at Boss and then looking over at me. He was sizing the situation up.

'"Go on in, Chewy," I said, "Boss wants to play with you. You'll like it." I said all kinds of encouraging things like that – my little sweetie, you beautiful dog, you, come on, honey – hoping he'd go in.

'He inched forwards but then he just stopped and looked at me, and then at Boss. But no, he was too smart. It was like he said: "You can't fool me, I'm smarter than that – I know that old trick."

'That drove me crazy. He wasn't interested in me, as a human being, he was oriented to my dog Boss – he just wanted to play with Boss,' Denise remembered.

'I wanted to rescue him so bad. He was so beautiful. But no, he was too smart. His street sense was his great protection.'

And now he's with us for two weeks. What a big treat, Denise thought to herself. She heard her husband walking into their kitchen; dinner was ready. Rob opened up the refrigerator door.

118

'He's not eating yet?' Rob asked.

Denise started to say, 'Oh no, he's eating' when she looked up from the dining-room table out into the back-yard: Chewy had disappeared. 'Apparently not.'

Where is he? she wondered.

'Oh, he's a smart one,' Denise said, 'I couldn't find him earlier. He was off hiding somewhere.' She looked back out the window: Chewy was still gone.

'You couldn't find him?' Rob questioned. He confidently walked out the kitchen onto the patio, scanning the backyard as he did so. 'How can we lose a big dog in our own backyard? Our yard isn't that big!'

Rob called Chewy. No response. He walked impatiently to the far side of the patio and called again. No response. 'Chewy, Chewy…'

'He's smarter than me,' Denise yelled. 'Come on in, dinner's ready. Bring their empty bowls, please.'

Coming back in and closing the kitchen door, Rob said: 'Apparently he's smarter than everyone.'

The backyard turned a blurry grey; the tree branches faded. 'I'm sure he's out there somewhere,' Denise insisted. They ate dinner and retired to watch TV.

The next morning, Chewy came and sat down next to Boss for their food. He looked eager.

'Oh, so you're hungry now,' Denise said. 'I'm glad to see you so hungry. Have I got treats for both of you!' she informed the dogs. Boss and Chewy sat side by side, like two brothers.

After breakfast when Denise came out with a leash and in her running shoes, Chewy stared at her inquisitively. He didn't run to hide this time. 'Oh, you're an inquisitive boy now,' she said. 'See my new shoes, we're going running. Boss can't come, but you can.' On hearing his name and noting the tone Denise gave him, Boss laid his head down on his paws. *This isn't fair*, he seemed to say.

'Mr Chewy, Boss has hip problems – he can't run. But Chewy, would you like to come?'

Actually you don't have a choice, Denise thought.

She leashed him and then led him out the front door and locked it. They walked three blocks over to the canal, where Denise began a slow jog. In the early morning air, she ran with Chewy along the canal path through dark shadows breaking into shining light, her breath panting, her left arm sticking out like a branch from her tree body so Chewy could adjust his stride to hers.

And he did easily: Chewy kept up with her. At times he jerked her arm, trying to mark some interesting object or sniff the earth or snort his nose among matted roots. He licked the black, tarred base of a telegraph pole. He'd walk along the base of the canal bank, bruising his shoulder up under the dark leaves of cottonwood branches sticking through fence slats to raise his back right leg, snuggle in a few small steps closer and mark his scent. From how he ran, Denise thought he knew this territory. And so he should for this was the exact same canal that Chewy had last made his home.

He ran beside Denise as if he'd jogged all his life. *Has he done this before?* she wondered. *He just adjusted to my stride so easily.* Just then Chewy jerked her arm again and dragged her towards the canal water.

'Where do you think you're going, Mr Chewy?' she asked.

Look at him, Denise said to herself, *he wants to sniff and mark everything. If I let him, he'd wade into the canal. He drinks from it – that can't be good for him. I bet the canal was one of his major sources of water when he was living on the streets. I bet there are all kinds of junk in that canal – pesticide runoff, stuff dumped in, who knows what?* She remembered the slimy gunk City workers pull out of the canal. *The canal can't be a safe place to drink water*, she told herself. *No drink for you, Mr Chewy. Not with me!*

'Have you figured this out, too?' Denise asked, pulling him back up from the canal water's edge. Chewy fought her, responding by pulling harder on his leash, leaning his weight in the direction of the water, his paws dug in. Denise couldn't figure out if it was the canal water he wanted, or simply to cool his hot paws in the cold water. Was this to be a contest of wills?

Denise and Chewy ran a mile in one direction, stopped briefly and rested. When Denise got up, she said: 'This is where we turn back, Chewy.' But Chewy pulled forwards hard, ignoring her. He seemed not only to want to go into the water but also to go further down the canal. Had he run down this way before?

Denise looked down the canal: nothing but canal and water, scrub brush and backyard fences. Then she realised it led back to Briggsmore Avenue. *Oh*, she thought to herself, *he's probably been down here before. It's like a passageway – a safe passageway around the city. Follow the canal and you won't get hit by cars.*

Not bad, Mr Chewy, she said to herself. Not a bad idea at all – he was full of surprises. They turned and ran back home along the canal.

Denise ran the canal nearest her home often. *Actually*, she thought, *I'm doing the same thing he does in using the canal for a safe activity: my running.*

As her running shoes crunched on the loose gravel, Chewy adjusted to her stride. Denise thought he'd probably run along this canal a lot. Suddenly her arm was yanked right – Chewy wanted to mark again. *Oh men*, Denise thought. Then the two of them jogged on; once off the canal embankment they walked home together.

Inside the house, changing her shoes Denise realised she had enjoyed her run with Chewy. He seemed to enjoy it too. But Denise had forgotten that the gardener came that day. He had given his key back to Denise and when he left after she'd gone for a run with Chewy, he hadn't been able to lock the gate. After the run, when she let the dogs outside in the yard, Chewy discovered the open gate.

Suddenly he was gone. Boss stayed in the yard but Chewy was already two blocks away, trotting towards Graceada Park, following scents he knew. Maybe the run with Denise had activated his curiosity and the need to explore. He was back to what he knew, in his neighbourhood; loose and exploring.

Denise didn't immediately notice that Chewy was gone. When she did realise, she was heartsick. What would Lauren think? *How could I be so stupid? How could the gardener not leave a note? He knew Boss was in the backyard.*

Luckily Boss didn't follow Chewy.

Chewy, dear Chewy, he might get killed. How will I find him? He can hide anywhere. Ugh, now he's gone, Denise thought, looking at the slightly open front gate. Lauren and Bruce will be crushed; *I'm* crushed. Denise stood in the front yard, worried, terrified, feeling guilty and looking wildly around for Chewy but he was nowhere to be seen.

So Denise got into her car and drove up and down all the streets near her house, up and down all the alleys. Then after an hour's search she pulled back into the alley leading to her garage.

There he was! Chewy was sitting in the shade near the front porch as if nothing had happened. *Apparently, Boss and food were the draw,* Denise thought.

Am I lucky or what? Oh, you're a good dog Chewy! Relieved he had decided to return, Denise couldn't believe her luck. After parking her car, she went inside the house and then came out the front door. She looked at Chewy, still sitting in the shade of a bushy plant: 'So you like it here?' she asked him.

Without hesitation, Chewy got up and trotted in through the front door as if nothing had happened. He looked at her after he got in the house as if to say, 'Thanks, that was fun. I'm glad to be back, though.' Denise shook her head. *What a dog*, she thought, *what a strange, magnificent dog. Lucky Boss was there!*

Little did she know that Chewy's escape from her house was to be the first of four escapes that would occur that year: Chewy was a hobo dog and also an escape artist.

At the end of the first week Denise took Chewy running with her again along the canal path (this time she made sure the gate was locked). Denise and Chewy ran the canal across streets, over bridges and around curves. Chewy ran with Denise like he'd found a home.

But a week later, Lauren knocked.

Chapter Thirteen
Welcome Home, Chewy

'Look,' Lauren said. She stood in the kitchen, looking at me. In a moment, she'd be going to Denise's to get Chewy. Now she wanted to show me Chewy's new gift.

Her hand held a beautiful new red/orange collar, dangling mid-air on the end of Chewy's leash. Lauren smiled at me.

'I bought him a new collar to match his coat.' Proud of herself, she did a little dance, spinning in a circle, her hands at her shoulders.

You're a dear, I thought to myself. I gave her a hug.

'Are you ready?' Lauren asked.

'As ready as I'll ever be.'

I can't lift twenty-five pounds, walk a mile or stop worrying about my health but hey, I'm alive! I thought.

Two weeks earlier, four weeks after her surgery, Lauren had asked her doctor if it would be wise for her to take care of Chewy. The doctor had looked at her as if she was from another planet. 'It would not be wise to take care of any new dog in your condition, let alone a large, sixty-pound dog,' he responded.

Now, after six weeks of recovery, she had healed enough. Right on schedule, according to her original plan: she had two more weeks at home before she had to go back to work. She would spend that time focusing on integrating Chewy into the household. The cats would be the biggest unknown. Cecelia, Gary, Lauren and I had discussed how Chewy might react to our cats. Chewy had a mild temperament so the odds were that he would adjust to the cats. But who knew? There was no guarantee. Living on the streets for a year and a half, he was semi-feral. We'd seen him interact with adults and their dogs, but never cats – they might appear to be snacks to him. Though a gamble, we'd bring him into our house and see what happened. If Chewy immediately chased or tried to kill any cat, we'd have to find him another home. Denise might take him. Or Cecelia, if nothing else worked out.

But what if at first he seemed OK and then two weeks later he killed one or more of the cats? What if he fought with just one particular cat? Or if one of them tried to eat his food, Chewy justifiably snapped at him and then accidentally killed or injured him? What, then? How would we feel? What would we do? Whose fault would that be? Could we risk any of our cats getting killed?

With Emma, our other, older dog, Chewy seemed fine. On the streets, she and Chewy just sniffed each other. When Chewy, being much younger, started playing and circling Emma, acting a little goofy, a little more aggressive, Emma jumped back, braced and growled a slow, low growl that said: 'Knock it off, I'm not interested'. Chewy soon got the message: just acquaintances, not friends.

Whatever information Emma picked up in the sniffing, she was not particularly interested in Chewy. At twelve years old, she didn't puppy play. Chewy's youthful energy just annoyed Emma.

We had hoped Chewy's energy might extend Emma's life by exercising her more – we'd read that sometimes happens. Any extra time with Emma would be a blessing.

But the cats! The cats were a different story.

* * *

When Lauren stepped out into the chilly March air to go to Denise's, I felt my stomach tighten. I imagined the worst but hoped for the best. Emma bumped up against my leg and stuck her head out the front door with me. We both watched Lauren walk down the street in her Keens, jeans and sweatshirt, with Chewy's red/orange leash slung over her shoulder. Emma looked up at me as if to say, 'What's she doing?' I shrugged my shoulders. All we could do was close the screen door and wait.

It was four weeks after my own medical procedure. Physically, I was healing but not completely healed – Lauren had to do any heavy lifting. Recently, she'd been able to start driving again, but I worried about her activity level. Any sudden strain could rip open her internal plumbing, ruin the operation and set us back seriously; equally if I did a bonehead sudden exertion, causing a relapse. I was to start a heart rehabilitation programme in two weeks, but I still didn't know my body's limits or trust it anymore. Healing would take time.

Watching Lauren, my mind wandered back over her operation: what she looked like coming out of anaesthesia, how bent over she'd been getting in and out of the car that first day, and now she was brazenly walking over to a bright new adventure.

As she rounded the corner, she stopped and waved back at us. I loved her brave soldier-on attitude but I could no longer be her backup, should things fall apart – my heart attacks had changed all that. I stood on the porch. Emma went back into the house.

Lauren's mother had driven us around during the two weeks when neither of us could drive. She had been cleaning the house and doing our shopping too. I knew she'd be over to see this new dog in a couple of days so we had a backup of sorts. As these thoughts squirrelled around my brain, I realised how chilled I was and that I needed to get inside the house. I was still having chest pains when I walked – no need to complicate things with more stupidity.

In the kitchen I checked on Emma. She'd gone back to her doggie bed in our bedroom and was licking on a bone. How would she react when Chewy entered her house? Chewy's new pristine bed was fluffed up and pushed back against the bedroom wall near Emma's. Sunlight darted back and forth across it. Outside the bedroom window, dried morning glory vines hung twining along the fence. *Another job for the spring*, I thought, which was just around the corner.

Out the bedroom window I could see Denise and Rob's Spanish-style house rise above our back fence. My studio behind our own house partially blocked my view. Lauren was probably talking to Denise right now, I thought. Boss and Chewy would be barking goodbye; Lauren leashing Chewy up. Once again Chewy had a big change in store for himself – poor guy!

First, he's drugged off the streets. Then he stays at the vet's, gets a series of shots and is neutered. Then off to Top Notch Kennels for two weeks with strange new people, strange smells he'd never known, dogs he'd never meet again. Now he's moved and meets his old friend Boss. Just as he's getting settled down to life with Boss – much better food, a new backyard and the fun of running along the canal with Denise – a strange but familiar-smelling woman comes and moves him again. How much can a dog put up with?

When will he get any peace?

I could imagine him a cartoon character, begging for mercy. On his back, his paws pounded the thin air for mercy, like Daffy Duck or Woody Woodpecker. Or talking to himself, like some Hamlet soliloquy: 'To Dog it or not to Dog it? That is the question.' Scared but free on the streets, or at the other end of a leash as Man's 'pet'?

Why don't they just leave me alone? I was hungry, yes. Cold and miserable in winter, yes. But I could wander the streets as I wished. I could follow the dog news in scents on trees, sniff telegraph poles and mark on bushes along the canal. Or follow the scents carried on the wind. I had dogs to play with, to chase along the canal; to make friends with. Now there is this new woman whose smells I vaguely remember, who is strapping me into a new collar and on a new leash and walking me over to a front door I've never smelled before. What's up with that? Give a dog a break! What's a dog to do? And what are these strange cat smells? I smiled to myself, imagining Chewy's plight and thinking about just how goofy I sometimes get.

In what seemed a minute or two, I heard the front door screen pulled open and then the turning click of the front door lock.

'Honey, we're home! Come on, Chewy.'

Suddenly, I heard the grating, scraping of Chewy's claws scratching across oak flooring. He was inside his new, hopefully permanent home.

'Hello, Chewy!' I shouted, elated as I walked from the kitchen into the living room. Lauren looked over at me, a mixture of concern and elation on her face. She closed the door.

'Finally,' she sighed, 'finally, we have him home.'

'So far, so good,' I said.

Her face beamed.

One weight lifted from her shoulders, another settling into place. One half of our adventure was done and now the other half began: transitioning Chewy to his new permanent home. Getting Chewy to bond with Lauren and me.

* * *

The day before, Lauren and I had spent an hour and a half crawling on our hands and knees in the backyard, checking our wooden fence for broken slats or loose boards. Chewy was smart – he'd be able to dig an escape hole under the fence or just squeeze his body through broken slats. I nailed any loose boards back into place. Several slats behind our garage were pulled loose – the fence posts wiggled when I pushed on them. I shored the post and slats up with two by fours. Both of us knew that if Chewy escaped or somehow got out then neither of us would be able to forgive ourselves, let alone have the energy to rescue him again.

In the living room, Chewy was shaking, panting rapidly and sniffing for scents. There were hundreds of new ones, I'm sure – cat smells, garlic and spices from cooking, remnants on the couch and furniture, paint smells, fresh flower scents from the roses on the dining-room table, dog and cat food in the utility room, lavender and lemon from the bathroom...

Lauren walked Chewy, still with the leash on, around the living room, letting him sniff the couch by the table, the TV and our other chairs. He glanced at me once or twice, his black dot eyebrows raising and dropping as he sniffed. When he came through the built-in sliding glass doors separating the living room from the dining room, he paused in the dining room and gave me a longer, intense sniff: first, my right knee, then a quick pass over my crotch. He stopped for a moment at my left knee and began licking my jeans. Why I didn't know, so I gently pushed his head away. Later, I figured out that I had wiped my hands on my jeans after eating salmon. He was on a royal sniffing tour!

Room by room, chair by chair, person by person, Chewy continued until he had had a first look and smell of our entire house. By the time he got into the kitchen Emma had come out of the bedroom to see what the strange noises were. She stopped suddenly and lowered her head. They sniffed each other curiously for a short time – Emma must have been wondering what Chewy was doing in her house, and why he wasn't out in the streets where she had first met him. In turn Chewy was most likely remembering Emma and her scent from the park.

Chewy was still panting, but not as frantically as when he'd first come into the house. He wasn't jumpy or especially nervous, just sniffing everything as he circled the rooms of our home. When Chewy got to the utility room, Lauren opened the back door, leaned over and unleashed him.

'This is your new home, Chewy,' she whispered in his ear. 'We hope you like it.'

Stunned, he stood in the doorway, looking out for the longest moment.

I thought he'd immediately jump out into the yard and run around, perhaps try to find an escape path. Instead, he simply stood still, his attention fixed on Fred and Fred's sidekick in crime, Pip.

Down the sidewalk leading to the back gate, Fred and Pip, two of our cats, sat motionless, glaring at Chewy. Who knew if they'd met before? Perhaps when Chewy had escaped from Denise's, he trotted across Pip or Fred. Both cats wandered our immediate neighbourhood during the daytime. Or maybe strange dogs had frightened them earlier in their lives. More likely, Chewy, a total stranger, had invaded their territory and they didn't like it – their focused glaring would have stopped anyone. Both watched Chewy intensely.

Fred is a very big cat. When I say big, I mean BIG – not fat, but big boned. He was nearly eighteen pounds of muscle. If he were human, he would have twenty-one-inch biceps with massive chest and shoulder development. I wish I had his physique! If he were a weight lifter, he could probably lift twice his body weight. Fred is all white. His personality and presence suggest he is of royal descent in the cat world. We frequently address him as 'His Majesty' or 'King Fred'. As he walks through the house at night, he sounds like a Mack truck rumbling down an alley. When he scratches on the back door at 3 a.m. to let us know he wants out to pee, we get up immediately. Like that Johnny Cash song – 'Nobody messes with a boy named Sue'. And nobody messes with a cat named Fred. Fred is not at all patient: when he wants something, he wants it 'now'.

Pip, on the other hand, is gentle and easy-going. He is a gorgeous Siamese but similar to Fred in that when he wants to go outside the house, he wants out now; he starts howling until we let him out. Like Fred, he is not patient and will not stop vocalising until his needs are met. Pip has the Siamese howl, which is like a siren. 'Pay attention,' the cry demands.

Fred and Pip both chose to live with us; we did not choose them. We are happy they joined our family but they most definitely chose us. They lived across the street in a household that did not allow cats inside their home. Apparently, Fred and Pip wanted more than they were receiving there.

A few years earlier, a scrawny stray appeared on our front porch. Lauren began leaving food for him. Pip and Fred discovered the food and began snacking there too. Soon both of them were walking inside our house, yet each night going home for their evening meal. After several months of slowly integrating themselves into our household, Lauren heard a knock at the front door. Julia, the neighbour's daughter, asked if Fred was in our house. When Lauren told her that he was, the girl asked for him.

Lauren promptly found Fred and placed him in the girl's arms in order for him to go home with her (Fred's owner Jennifer was waiting patiently for him across the street).

When home, Fred looked up at the woman who owned him, looked out across the street at Lauren, then he wriggled out of his owner's arms and bolted across the street past Lauren to disappear into the bushes of our front yard. Jennifer looked stunned: clearly Fred had voted with his paws.

'I'm sorry,' Lauren said, her heart aching. She knew Fred had a better life with us but she couldn't ask them to give him up; he was a special cat. 'I'll go get him.'

'Nah,' the woman said. 'You can have him – he voted with his feet.'

Her daughter Julie shouted, 'He must really love you.' She smiled and closed the door.

I was standing on the front porch, watching.

'Did you see that?' Lauren asked, a little stunned.

I smiled.

Just then, Pip dashed back across the street too. We opened the front door and both Fred and Pip bolted in. When we both looked back at the door where the woman had been standing, she had gone inside. Their TV was blaring.

'Well,' Lauren said, 'I guess we officially have two new cats.' Fred was purring at her feet.

'Beats me,' I said. 'I thought I'd painted over that invisible sign on the house that says, "All cats check this house out. They are suckers in this house for needy animals. They will take care of you".' Somehow this reminded me of the Underground Railroad during slavery.

I was thinking this while standing behind Chewy as he looked out the door towards Fred and Pip: it was do or die, right now. If Chewy chased them, he was history. Top Notch and the vet bills came to $2,000. Lauren had invested that money on a calculated hope that Chewy would adapt successfully but who really knew?

Fred knew.

* * *

In one decisive action Fred set Chewy straight, absolutely straight. In no uncertain terms, straight – straight about who was boss, how Chewy was to behave with the cats and what the repercussions would be if he didn't. Pip covered Fred's back as his faithful partner. Right from their first meeting, the ground rules were set.

Chewy stepped out the back door onto our small back porch. It was showdown at the O.K. Corral. It was Wyatt Earp and Doc Holliday with the Earp brothers versus the Clantons and the McLaurys. It was his whiteness, the Terminator, as Great White Cat coming to give Chewy an attitude adjustment.

Fred, with Pip following him, walked straight up the sidewalk, big white paw by big white paw. Two cat gunslingers, *High Noon* had nothing on these two cats. Not knowing what to expect, Lauren and I went outside and stood nearby, trying to welcome Chewy to his safe new environment. *Safe?*

Chewy stared directly at Fred. I could hear the surround-sound movie music playing in the background inside my head.

Watching Fred advance on Chewy, Lauren had decided to let the animals work it out. It was a gutsy decision – if some type of fight developed then we were there to stop it, hopefully. Lauren was sure that she could; I wasn't so convinced.

I would have intervened because I worried Chewy might attack Fred. He certainly outweighed him: his teeth were much bigger, claws longer and his neck fur offered thicker protection. And he must have been a couple of hundred times stronger than Fred, even with Pip's backup. Realistically, I figured if Fred or Pip deeply angered Chewy, then with one bite he could end things quickly. But I was a novice at these sorts of decisions and Lauren had much more experience. And better judgement, I hoped. And I hoped Chewy did too.

But Chewy lacked one thing: Fred was on his home territory.

Fred seemed to be saying, 'Who is this big, dumb dog who dares come into this house, uninvited? Who does he think he is? What mind-boggling audacity of this creature to think he can just waltz into my territory!'

Fred was the dominant cat, and the biggest one too. Now that Morris was gone, he was also the most streetwise. Both Fred and Pip had chosen to live in our house. They were not going to tolerate newcomers, or at least they would set Chewy straight regarding decorum around cats.

Fred and Pip stopped walking perhaps six inches from Chewy's nose. Chewy could have guessed or known he was being challenged but I think he just wondered what the heck was going on. *What is this new yard and who are these two scary cats?* Chewy moved his head a fraction of an inch forward – a gesture, I think, just to sniff.

That's when Fred popped Chewy on the nose not once, not twice, but three or four eye-blinkingly fast times. Swats that stunned Chewy. They didn't turn his head, they didn't knock teeth out but they weren't love taps. These were 'Do I have your attention now?' swats.

Before he could jump back, before the shock wore off and the pain settled in, when the speed and quickness were still sending electrical and chemical messages up Chewy's neural connections through his nose to his forebrain, Chewy reflexed and pulled back. His eyes widened when the synapses circuitry in his hypothalamus lit up the brain cells that read in big white letters: 'Don't mess with the Cats!'

Fred stepped back and Pip stepped forwards simultaneously. Then Pip followed up with three or four quick swats of his own, as if to say: 'Did you get that, big guy?'

Poor Chewy!

I cringed, and involuntarily lifted my hands in self-defence.

Fred and Pip were a one-two combination of intimidation. Just a little painful nose scratching to get Chewy's attention, to quickly and relatively painlessly establish who was boss; who you didn't mess with. The species message was: 'Whoever you are, never ever, ever chase, hurt or kill a cat. Got that?'

In college at U.C. Berkeley, I briefly sparred with the college boxing team. I've worked out on speed bags and have seen fast 'cat-like reflexes'; I've watched Bruce Lee, fast Kung Fu masters and Shaolin priests stun with their phenomenal speed and punching abilities. And I've seen Sugar Ray Leonard's speed and jab combinations beat a cut into a bloody pulp.

But Fred was simply in another league and Chewy knew it. And so he turned, ducked under the handrail by the back steps, stepped off the back porch and backed up along the sidewalk towards my studio, his eyes riveted on Fred. Chewy didn't seem terrified; he didn't even seem frightened – he seemed not to understand why what was happening was happening – but he clearly got Fred and Pip's message. And until he figured out the situation, he was playing it safe and backing off. *Who were these guys anyway?* he seemed to say. But he was staying clear until he had figured them out.

He was, after all, brand new to the household – alone in the wilderness, like Moses. Trying to figure out the rules – the natives' customs, the house etiquette, the species and household pack rules.

Fred would have none of it. You've probably seen pictures of body builders when they puff their chests out and up, suck in their stomachs, put their hands on their waists and spread their lat muscles – they look massive. Some of them truly are: 250 to 300 pounds of rock-hard muscle, just huge.

Fred did a cat version of that when he puffed himself up and braced his shoulders. With a swagger, he walked aggressively towards Chewy, one paw step at a time.

Watching Fred, I had never seen anything vaguely resembling such aggressive actions. He reminded me of a mountain gorilla's protective dominance minus the leaf and branch throwing. What does that mean? He had the towering effect of a rogue killer, a cat that was a cross between King Kong and Godzilla.

Fred backstepped Chewy down the sidewalk past the studio, behind the house, turning him right and backing him up onto the gravel path along the side of our house towards our front gate. It was breathtaking: thirty dangerous feet of sheer dominance. When he had Chewy backed up against the gate, Fred stopped and sat down for a moment. He let Chewy stew. Chewy, meanwhile, hadn't taken his eyes off Fred. Then Fred deliberately sat down in the middle of the path and began cleaning his paws, one at a time, as if to say, 'Move and this is what I have for you, Big Guy.'

By this time Lauren decided to intervene. She wanted Chewy to learn the cat rules, but she didn't want him hurt or permanently terrified. I was right behind her.

When Fred felt he had made his point, he suddenly spun around and walked away, never looking back. Chewy was stunned. He sat down before the gate for the longest time. I wondered what was going on inside his mind. Was it something like, 'What the hell was that?', 'Who is that white guy?' or even 'I want outta here, now!'?

Stunned, he got the message.

Our other cats were in the house almost as if it was too terrifying to watch. Fred and Pip walked past Lauren and me, their rumps pumping as they walked with what appeared to be an absolute conviction that they had behaved appropriately and wisely. Lauren chuckled in amusement at what she thought was these two with their BIG personalities. I wasn't too sure – the brutality and speed of the swats, the backing up of Chewy into the front gate, the whole interaction upset me. I knew I was probably projecting – that behaviour was probably a normal part of the everyday animal world – but still it upset me. I wanted to comfort Chewy but I really didn't know how.

We then went to reassure Chewy as best we could that he had not just entered cat hell for all time. Surprisingly, he wasn't trembling, or didn't dash sideways along our redwood fence to dodge our outreached hands trying to pet him. He didn't bark or whine; his eyes followed ours. When I buried my hand in his neck fur, saying, 'Chewy, Chewy, Chewy, it's all right, honey,' he just glanced at me quickly and then turned away. His body swayed gently as Lauren and I uttered what we thought would be soothing reassurance from us, trying to let him know he was safe. But I have no confidence that anything we did comforted him. In those few moments before we gave up I felt the great distance between our species, the silence and the loneliness between us.

Later, the next day, when we looked at Chewy's nose it was laced with a few tiny superficial scratches: painful-looking but nothing life threatening or needing a vet's care. Fred could easily have ripped Chewy's nose to shreds, had he wanted to. But all he wanted to do was establish boundaries, and that was what he had done. Brilliantly, we guessed, because even Lauren and I were also a bit more wary of Fred after this display. When we picked him up and he was moody or feisty, we put him down again quickly. In one magnificent display, he'd trained us too. Fred was the 'Alpha Cat' in our house (probably our block too and maybe even the city).

From that day forwards Chewy left the cats alone. Particularly Fred and Pip.

Chapter Fourteen
Chewy's First Struggles

After Fred's big paw swatted him, the rest of Chewy's first week was dull. Fred remained the enforcer – Fred's paw swinging in the air after Chewy's face occurred several more times. Each was a fast swipe several inches from Chewy's nose. By the end of the first week, Chewy had gone through his new house initiation – a dog hazing, if you will – that set cat boundaries. Chewy funnelled his stressed-out energy into searching for escape routes.

'Look at this,' I said, pointing to a shallow dugout hole, and Lauren joined me by the air-conditioning unit. Smooth as a blanket, four inches deep, Chewy had scratched out a little sink-hole observation post. Hidden behind a jade tree, he scraped out all the debris – dry, rotted, clotted-up leaves, broken twigs and fallen black-spotted orange tangelos from our backyard tree. Chewy had created a secret resting place for himself. Hidden in plain view, a glance, even a scrutinising study, would fail to spot him.

Most likely he had created similar safe holes in the past. He had recreated what a year and a half of living on the streets had taught him worked: protect your back, stay low, hidden by bushes on three sides with a clear view of anyone or anything approaching. Don't spies do the same thing? They sit with their backs to the furthest wall allowing them to completely observe the actions of others. Chewy, the spy, was taking care of himself.

During the day, while the sun threw dark shadows over him, Chewy could glance over the entire backyard from his ground-level perspective. He had two observation posts set up, one by the air-conditioning unit and the other by my studio. Perhaps all his future escapes were quietly planned there. These dugouts gave him a clear view of the exits – the hole by the air-conditioning unit afforded a view of the back gate, while the hole by my studio gave a view of the front gate.

The gates squeaking hinges alerted him to their opening and closing. Whenever Lauren or I opened the back gate, Chewy's wrinkled nose was right there, sniffing the fence, his head pushing on the redwood slats. Ready to slip into the alley.

When my fingers slipped the lock from the latch at the front gate, Chewy's head lifted up from the hole he'd dug by the studio. He watched the movement of my hands, heard the lock click open. When he came quickly running up the gravel path to the gate, I had to gently push against his flank to get him to retreat even a few paces.

Chewy's desire seemed clear: he wanted out of the gates, out to the world he was familiar with. He wanted to explore the alley's rank odours, poke his nose into spilt garbage dropped by the ton-and-a-half automated garbage truck each Thursday, and to lick the oily stench on the green bin by the gate.

When he came running up to the front gate, did he want out? Did he simply want to frolic, carefree, in the front yard while I washed my car? In his first few weeks I couldn't risk finding out. Nor could Lauren.

Lauren and I discovered rich evidence of Chewy's continued investigations: the redwood fence covered with persistent scratches, powdery dirt clawed back below where the fence planks kissed the ground, small little hills of dirt, leafy refuse and fuzzy roots dug up in piles along the back fence out of view and by my studio, an outpost giving him a clear view of the opening and closing of the front gate.

When Chewy rested in the front room, he always sat within a few feet of the front door. His eyes were always on the door. To me, he seemed to be casing the front door for the possibility of escape – subtly but relentlessly.

Our front door consists of a series of fifteen small windows – three across, five down – all framed in painted wood. With the curtains up, Chewy had a full view of the front yard and street. Two narrow windows on either side of the door expanded his view. As he sat on the floor, I often sat beside him rubbing his back, massaging along his spine. He would throw his head back, mouth open in a smile, and roll his head back and forth, watching me.

I would tell him how much I loved him, how fine a young man he was, but the minute someone came to the front door – for example, the mailman – his eyes were there. I would get up on my feet to open the door, but blocking his exit, often saying, 'No, Chewy, stay. STAY!' Sometimes he got up and I had to push him back with my thigh, or leg, or ask Lauren to take him away from the door. I'm sure the sudden shift between tone and body language confused him.

Lauren would say, 'Look, he's panting.' Chewy would lie back down on his side, four legs out before him, head resting on our oak floor and close his eyes, then exhale what almost seemed a sigh of resigned sadness. Then his panting would start.

At first, Lauren thought Chewy was overheated. With his thick fur we had to make sure he stayed cool. Was he panting to cool himself down? But then we noted he panted when it wasn't particularly hot. In the evenings he panted, lying on his dog bed. This panting became one sign of the stress Chewy was experiencing in adjusting to his last new home, the unfamiliar.

If Fred set the tone for Chewy's behaviour with cats and reinforced the rules, our other cats seemed to sleep through his arrival. Gracie occasionally ate his wet food until the day Chewy snapped at her. In the early morning he plopped himself beside his stainless steel food bowl outside my studio door. Flies swirled straight up into the warm spring air. Our other sly-eyed cats inched forwards on their bellies, their noses working hard, sniffing the scents of Chewy's wet food. Deceptively suggesting they were, after all, only stretching before going back to sunning themselves. But Chewy gave them something to remember: he leaned his spotted muzzle forwards and snapped several times in rapid succession at the imaginary black flies buzzing in the air. His limits subtly displayed, he lay down and relaxed. This guarded loafing seemed to say: 'Don't mess with my food'.

Perhaps his tongue licking the brown lumps of wet food conveyed the message, better than barking, who could eat what and when: Chewy slowly rising to his full height, his ears twitching off irritating flies, his dark head lowering into his shiny food bowl, his jaws chomped on hard biscuits broken in two by Lauren or me. Pushing his white paws into the cement, his spinal cord stretched from his shoulders down through his powerful back. Watching, the cats knew how the strength he possessed could easily be turned on them should they fail to respect the boundaries he set around his food. Happily, after Chewy negotiated these boundaries, the cats soon respected them. In the evening when Chewy's dinner food was given to him, the cats patiently watched, wide-eyed. Eventually, they turned towards their own food waiting for them in their individual brightly coloured bowls: the heaven of Chewy's food was his and his alone.

Habitually, Chewy stood a few feet away from the bottom step of our back door. He let Emma, Fred and Pip enter first. The other cats eased up to Chewy, curling their tails around his mane, rubbing their bodies along his flank and stepping forward beneath his neck in what I took to be homage. Some nights at dusk, the cats wouldn't come in until Chewy went in. Other nights if he plopped down in the bushes when called, wanting to lay outside in the cooler night air, the other cats cluttered beside him. Never Fred or Pip, but the rest of the cats seemed to love Chewy. 'Love' isn't a word I use loosely – perhaps they merely respected the fact that he was bigger, stronger and most likely capable of killing any or all of them. But as I stood in the back door frame watching the cats and Chewy interact, a feeling in my bones, a certain kind of conviction hard to articulate, overcame me that some kind of emotional bond had grown between them.

Maybe his gentleness won them over. Perhaps we're clueless to the deeper meaning of their interactions but during those first few weeks, Chewy made his peace with our cat family, one of his new animal families.

Relations with his second family, our older dog Emma, were straightforward enough: Emma ate first, Emma walked out the front door first, Emma chose which dog bed she wanted each night and Emma entered the bedroom first. Clearly, she was dominant. But in the backyard garden, Emma loosened up: she plopped her belly down on the grass, watching Lauren gardening in the yard. But Chewy was younger and curious: he pushed his nose against and into the wheelbarrow, sniffing the pulled dry sunflower stalks, the weeds and the dropped rotten oranges. He also followed Lauren to the back gate.

Emma's seeming indifference must have disappointed Chewy for he loved to play – he still had that wonderful adolescent energy at a year and half of age. In the first few weeks, when we walked Chewy with Boss, Chewy and Boss were inseparable play pals. But at least Emma and Chewy were at peace.

* * *

Now that we guessed Chewy wouldn't kill the cats, nor injure them, and he also rubbed along with Emma, would Chewy bond with Lauren and me? And if so, how long would it take?

Lauren's fantasy of bonding with Chewy was this: Chewy would bark and protect her. Chewy would follow her around the back or front yard while she gardened. He would listen to her talk, to whatever she said, as if she were brilliance herself, or at least interesting. Chewy would go for long walks with her. He would sit quietly while she sorted her mail and watched a TV movie. She could rub him and hug him, and grab him by his ears, looking him in his eyes, and then kiss him on the snout.

By contrast I hadn't given bonding much thought. I had first seen Chewy, but I'd always thought of him as a dog for Lauren – I assumed Chewy would just bond with Lauren as the alpha dog, and I wanted Lauren to be happy with Chewy. Yet Chewy's beauty gave me pleasure. His gentleness intrigued me as I had sensed 'something' in his eyes beyond sadness – an intelligence; a strength of character I wondered about. A passing glint in Chewy's eyes left me puzzled: who was this dog, and what were his possibilities?

I didn't see that 'something' always but it was there; in the early afternoon on a hot day when Chewy was lying on the door to the cellar, a look of utter boredom on his face from being stuck in a small fenced-in backyard. The look that said, 'Oh, please can't we go out, I'm dying in here!' And I would swear there was intelligence behind that look. Or when Chewy had finished playing with Boss and he came over to Lauren and me and rolled over, up on his back, legs kicking in the air, head tossed back, tongue flicking out the side of his smiling mouth, his eyes lost in doggie nirvana. I would swear there was something there: happiness and something else. Something like contact between species, a wild 'I'm happy, really happy and thank you for being my companion'.

These feelings intrigued me – I wanted to know more about them. They reminded me of experiences I'd had while drawing models, or of times when I had taught art to developmentally disabled adults and they had taught me so much about courage and character and the shallow limits of verbal communication.

I wondered whether Chewy would bond with me to some extent too. What lessons could I learn from a free-thinking stray who had lived on the streets for a year and a half, from puppyhood until young adulthood?

Chapter Fifteen
We Have Work to Do!

If Donna Soderstrom, the dog trainer, knew anything about dogs, she knew when a dog had bonded with a family. And Chewy hadn't.

A few weeks after he entered our household Lauren contacted Donna about working with Chewy on one-on-one training sessions. We knew he would need special training due to his circumstances.

During the first session Chewy came out of the dining room only after repeated calls. His eyes quickly glanced around the living room as if sizing up everyone. Who was this stranger with the imposing stance, with the confidence of an alpha dog? Bruce and Lauren, he knew. With the two cats Fred and Pip he was negotiating a sort-of peace. But the little woman with new perfume odours he studied cautiously. 'Who was she? What did she want?' his eyes seemed to say.

Chewy sat down on his hind legs, front paws forwards, settling his chest on the oak flooring. He yawned, turning his head, and tucked it away from this stranger in studied disregard. Had he been an adolescent boy, which he was in dog years, you might have thought he was acting incredibly bored yet was nervously alert.

Donna, Lauren and I as the adults in the room looked at each other, then smiled. Like the parents of a misbehaving adolescent, we expected better behaviour from Chewy. *He's got balls*, I thought. *He's rude*, Lauren thought. *Yep, he needs training*, Donna thought. *It's obvious he hasn't bonded with them – I've got my work cut out for me.*

Those years in the street had taught Chewy street smarts but not living-with-people smarts. Donna reviewed what Lauren and I had told her about Chewy: a year and a half living on the street as a puppy, shy, extremely gentle, friendly with dogs but very wary of people, easily frightened and basically now hiding under bushes in their backyard. Doesn't come in when called, refuses to eat for days at a time and lives for his walks. Initially terrorised by Fred and Pip, he now gets along with cats but still extremely skittish. The prognosis was par for the course given his history but full of hope. *Four new homes in six weeks – that's a lot of adjustments in a short period of time*, thought Donna. *If he has already made some adjustments then he might accept his new life, permanently.*

I like his 'show me' attitude, Donna thought to herself.

'You're right,' she told Lauren, 'he's beautiful.'

'Chewy,' Donna said with quiet authority. She moved closer to him. 'Chewy,' she said again, now standing directly in front of him. Lying quietly a few feet from her, Chewy looked at her and then at Lauren and again turned his head away.

'Can you put a leash on him?' Donna said to Lauren, who did so and then passed it to Donna. Donna walked Chewy around the couch three times. He followed easily, though he repeatedly glanced up at Lauren or me, seemingly for reassurance. The slightest thing – a noise, a sudden cat movement, a phone ringing – easily distracted him. When Chewy sat down, Donna stopped directly in front of him.

'Chewy,' she said, 'Good dog. Chewy, good dog.' He looked directly at her.

While she looked at him, Donna told Lauren, 'I'm going to try to teach him a few things.'

She tried to teach him three or four times to sit, using persuasive treats, but each time Chewy simply gazed back at her as if he didn't comprehend or, most likely, didn't care to understand.

Finally, at the end of the first session, Donna put her hand out to stroke his head, saying 'Good dog, Chewy', but he moved his head so her hand was petting empty air.

'Well,' Donna said, 'it's too early for training. He has not bonded with you. We will not be able to train him until he has bonded more to you both. Maybe, in a few months, he'll be ready – he is not ready now.'

When Chewy heard her voice, he cocked his head and then looked at her as if to say, 'You got that right, if I'm still here...' We would shortly find out what that look meant.

Lauren thought what Donna recommended made sense: Chewy had not bonded with us. Frustrated and sad, she looked over at me and thought to herself, it will take time. She was again reminded of how her expectations were so distorted – when she tamed feral cats the process could be lengthy. Why had she expected it to be any different with Chewy? *Because he is a dog*, she thought to herself. *Dogs are social, they are pack animals.*

Rescuing Chewy was her first experience of rescuing a semi-feral dog.

In a few months, when Donna returned, would our relationship with Chewy have changed? We didn't know what he had in store for us, what the signs of ready were. But we were about to learn the hard way.

Chewy's journey involved small steps. First, recovering from the stress and shock of leaving the street and enduring four new homes in six weeks. Second, crazy as this may seem to attribute to a dog, he had to willingly leave behind his street life, the positives and the negatives. Third, Chewy had to bond with his new family. Bonding meant adapting to a new dog, some strange cats and two caring but confused human beings.

Chapter Sixteen

The Great Escape

Still, Chewy lay in his shallow command post, his view-point an easy 180 degrees of the backyard, safe from any predators' surprise or attack. His foxhole; his safety net.

Some nights Chewy simply refused to come into the house. Who knew why? Most likely he was reverting to what he was comfortable with, being outside. After all, why would anyone sleep inside a house?

'Chewy,' Lauren called into the darkness beyond the back-door light.

'Chewy, Chewy!' Desperation and disappointment blended in her voice. She turned to me in the kitchen – 'See if you can get him to come in.' She walked back into the house, grabbed a kitchen towel and began drying the cat bowls. Just then Fred walked in; the other cats were already inside, eating their late-night snacks. I went out the back door to find Chewy.

I walked along the raised beds in the backyard, past cherry tomatoes in blossom; sheaths of courgette leaves layered, twisted and spun around the birch brown supports. Watermelon tendrils laced into wire supports.

I stopped at the edge of the gravel path and shouted Chewy's name into the night sky. Nothing. Then I hollered his name again.

I felt like a wolf vainly baying at the moon – 'Chewy, Chewy...' *What's up with that dog?* I wondered. In a slow deliberate voice, carefully articulating each vowel and letter, I uttered 'Chew-wiiii-eee' like an auctioneer shouting 'sueie' at a cattle market.

Still nothing. In the cooling April night air a circle of small fluttering moths tossed themselves at the porch light. Spinning around on my heels, I walked back along the gravel path and rambled over towards the air-conditioning unit. Hidden back in the bushes, I thought I could see Chewy's eyes glowing yellow in the darkness. Suddenly light from the porch reflecting off his retina turned Chewy eyes luminous. *That's eerie*, I thought, *I'm glad he's not a wolf.*

'Chewy,' I said, hunching forwards, hand outstretched. 'Come on, Boy, we just want you to come in.'

Nothing appeared to coax him. Then where the fallen cactus careened over the now-damp ground cover, Chewy's paw appeared tentatively and then his body pushed through the green cradling leaves. Chewy came out towards me with his head down, then up, looking at me like he expected the ritual of hand stroking along his head. He stopped when I said: 'Good boy, Chewy! Good boy, we were worried about you. Come on, come here, fellow.'

Chewy walked closer, allowing himself to be petted. Holding his body slightly sideways, he dropped his shoulders with each gentle petting, each stroke of my hand comforting him, until he began to raise his body into the hand strokes, into the loving caresses, the warm waiting hands telling him he was a wonderful dog.

'Yes, yes, there you are, Chewy. You're a wonderful dog!' I exclaimed. This slow ceremony under the stars crossed over some kind of bridge between species. Call it trust for a moment, as Chewy and I both planted our feet on the sidewalk and walked, dog following man, into the open back door.

'Great! You got him to come in,' Lauren smiled, still drying dishes and beginning to pick up the three cat food containers. 'Nice to see you, Chewy – nice to have you in the house for the night,' she said lovingly and perhaps a bit sarcastically. She put one container away and then walked over to the hallway door. Her hand opened it: 'Here, Chewy, you can go lay down on your bed.'

Without a sound, Chewy scooted around her body and disappeared behind the hallway door, his tail now arched up and flaring.

'Well, that's a miracle,' Lauren said, smiling at me. 'How'd you do that?'

'Beats me,' I replied. 'Beats me.'

But other nights Chewy refused still to come in. No special pleading changed his mind. Some nights it was cooler outside under the stars, not so boring as being in a house. Then again, some nights the hum of the kitchen refrigerator, the clang of dishes and Fred or Pip always lurking in the background would scare anyone off.

Outside, the freedom of the shadows, birds chirping, the early-morning fog in the bushes and the scents from over the fence reminded Chewy of his lost world that he knew was still out there. In the shade of the orange tree with its sweet smells he could plan, or dream of escape. Or perhaps even of staying. He might be warming to these two humans yet – who knew?

Progress with Chewy seemed slow; trust was built in little pieces and easily destroyed. Lauren, trying to help Chewy feel safe, comfortable and loved, had to remind herself that he was adjusting to a whole new world. After all, he had spent the majority of his young life on the streets.

In his scouting of our house, Chewy discovered that as at Rob and Denise's there were three ways out: the front door, the front gate and the back gate. In an attempt to get out he had scraped pieces of mahogany wood off the front door of Rob and Denise's house. He had left his mark – no way out there.

Chewy had meticulously sniffed the front gate, watched the gardener come and go with his machines that whirled and popped grass out its side. And he lay on the gravel path by my studio and listened to the hinge lock on the front gate open and click closed. He knew what the sounds told him: when it was open, he could escape and when it was closed and locked, he couldn't. But it was the front door that interested him most.

The front door in the front room by the big-screen TV. He sprawled out on the wood floor before the TV on those evenings when his two humans watched those noisy movies with the surround sound. The speakers hurt his ears but he had already learned to adjust. His eyes quietly studied how these humans moved in their front room. How when Fred scratched at the lower front door glass pane, one of them got up, turned the door knob to pull it open and pushed the screen perhaps six inches so that Fred in all his whiteness could slither out the door into the night air. Or how when Pip's face appeared outside the door, crying and meowing to come in, one of them got up and let him in. The door was left hanging open again. Through his studies Chewy became a doggie James Bond with anticipated escape and tricks up his paw.

Not that Lauren or I'd notice. Transfixed by the surround sound on the widescreen TV, with its high-tech special effects vision, we were quietly preoccupied with the plot.

Lauren sat balancing her chequebook, with a cat on her lap. Meanwhile I googled the universe on my laptop while multi-tasking: searching for art and health topics on the computer, looking at the movie on the big screen. Both our attentions were preoccupied and divided.

In the late afternoons, Chewy carefully scrutinised how I checked for mail. How my sloppy routine presented his greatest opportunity: the slow opening of the locked wooden door, the unhinging of the screen door flip-hook lock, the screen door's hinges squeaking open. How I reached up with my right-hand fingers above my head and locked the screen in place while I casually leaned on my right leg, looking out to see if there was any mail deposited in the mailbox in the front of the house. The foot-wide hole I left by my left side was the space a hippopotamus could squeeze through, Chewy thought: an escape route.

Chewy squinted from his floor perch in the living room, watching the screen door open and that big gaping hole get wider and wider. He lay on the floor attempting to estimate exactly how long it would take him to lunge through it into freedom. And what if I resisted? What if I tried to stop him? How would I stop him? Or what if I suddenly slammed the screen door shut? Could he afford a mistake? What would happen then?

Infatuated with the breath of freedom he smelt, Chewy studied my mistakes: my careless trusting, my human form slipping in and out of the screen door, sometimes pausing to look up and down the street, or shouting hello to a neighbour, or simply gazing up at the canopy of tree branches twisting like tendrils into the sky. Should he rise too late the door would slam in his face and I might surmise his intent.

* * *

Of course, we are not sure if Chewy imagined or planned his escapes, or if his actions were just a spontaneous reaction to an opportunity presented to him. All we know is that he watched for a number of days. Then one day his body formed a ferocious lunge that became his first escape.

When it happened I was off balance. Faster than even he anticipated, Chewy lunged through the door opening, slamming his body through. My body slammed Chewy's shoulder with a thigh block much weaker than he expected. But Chewy's lunge, driven by a piercing determined drive, burst through all of my scrambling opposition into the sun and freedom of the front yard.

Before I could shout 'NO!' Chewy was gone. He ran down the front porch and past my truck parked in the driveway onto the sidewalk and to freedom. Halfway down the block, he stopped and turned his head over his shoulder to look back at my stunned expression as I stood in the open front door.

I shouted, 'No, Chewy, don't!'

When I lifted my right foot up to step off the porch Chewy turned and ran. His trot, swollen with fear, sped up and seemed to lengthen with each stride. Down the street he went, cutting between cars, jumping over yard refuse raked to the kerb, and then he bolted straight for the canal.

* * *

Her phone rang.

Lauren sat at her desk, letting the phone ring. She glanced at the caller ID number. Out of her window a truck rattled down the street as two pedestrians in black suits walked across the plaza and disappeared into the parking lot beside her office. She glanced at her watch, 10.30 a.m., and then she picked up the phone and said: 'Hi, honey.'

'Chewy escaped,' my voice gasped. Beneath my words Lauren could feel me bracing against her anticipated silence, against her stunned response.

'Escaped?' she questioned 'How could he escape?'

This came at exactly the wrong time, she thought, *right in the middle of a busy schedule on a very busy day.* Lauren looked across her desk piled high with pending audits, department projects and work to be completed. Her computer screen was tagged with post – it's like a crossword puzzle. She reached behind the framed picture of herself and Emma for the photo of me leaning against an oak tree in the High Sierra. *That's my man*, she thought. She put the photograph down.

'What happened?' she asked.

'He bolted out the front door while I was reaching for the mail. He ran down the street. He's gone. I'm going to go looking for him. Can you come?'

'Look,' she said, 'this is a bad time, I have a meeting in a few minutes.'

I felt a cold numbness climbing up my ribs into my chest cavity as Lauren spoke. *She's about to hang up*, I thought. I closed my eyes waiting for the click and deep dial tone.

'Maybe I can get away for an early lunch around 11.30, after my meeting, but definitely not now. You'll have to deal with it until I can get away. Can you go look for him? Remember to take the leash.'

As Lauren put the phone down she thought to herself, *Bruce is a good man. He certainly loves Chewy and accidents do happen. Sometimes, though*! Images of Harry Potter characters, Harry and Hermione, flowed through her head. She remembered an early dialogue from the series when Hermione comments to herself about Harry, 'What an idiot!' in her upper-crust, highly contemptuous voice. As she thought of this, she pictured me.

'OK,' I said, putting the phone down. I looked out the front door of our house and wondered what to do next. Already I knew the answer. It was one of my worst fears – I had lost Chewy and I was responsible. I should take Lauren's advice and start looking for Chewy until she was able to get here. A car drove by, with two riders hunched low in the front seats. In the distance a dog barked. I squinted down the block wondering for a moment where Chewy would have run.

'God, I hope he doesn't get himself killed,' I said out loud.

* * *

Chewy was out of breath with aching chest muscles when he felt the alley weeds brush against his body. He climbed up through them onto the hard packed earth of the embankment. Flies and gnats swarmed before his face. He climbed to the top of the embankment and stood for a moment, his face bathed in sunlight. The scents from the splashing canal water and flowering eucalyptus tree filled his nostrils. He felt safe now. For a moment he snapped at a dragonfly. Snap, snap! Two more misses.

Fragrances galore: odours of thistle, dog root and sweet bunched blossoms from a yard across the canal. The gravel pathway along the top of the embankment stank with dried cat scat and fresh droppings from dogs. To Chewy, these scents were heaven.

So who were these new dogs? Who owned these fresh spray marks? Chewy wandered down the slope of the embankment to sniff a tree trunk, then he raised his leg and marked over it. He circled and came back for a second, higher attempt. Satisfied, he scratched the dried leaves into the earth to spread the scent from the pads under his paws. Then he walked twenty feet down the fence into the shade of a palm tree.

Free again, he rested in the shadows. Minutes later he got up. If he were human, he might have tried to get as much distance between himself and the house as possible. Or he could have simply hidden out until dark and then taken off. But Chewy merely jaunted down the canal.

* * *

Back at the house, I stood in the living room bent over, chin to knee, before the front door Chewy had recently barged through. I was distraught. As I tied the shoelaces of my Nike walking shoes, one at a time, I stared out the screen door. Our neighbour Patty, across the street, stood watering her front lawn. I admired her. Even though she had multiple sclerosis she hadn't let her disease stop her. *What guts*, I thought.

I had decided even though it was probably hopeless that I would search for Chewy for an hour. After that he was on his own until Lauren came home. I had gone inside to get my mobile phone. When I stepped out onto the porch and turned to lock the front door, Patty waved and yelled, 'Going for a walk?'

Grasping the doorknob tightly, I tried skilfully to slip my key into the upper lock in one quick motion, but of course I missed. My hands felt like oversized stumps. The screen door bounced against my back. Touching the keyhole with one finger, I slid the thin key along the side of my finger for guidance. The key slipped in effortlessly. Then I turned to Patty and shouted, 'Chewy got out. I've got to go find him. Have you seen him?'

Her lips let out a low moan. 'Oh no,' she said simultaneously turning off the water. 'You can kiss him goodbye if you don't get him soon – he'll be out of the state before you know it. That's terrible. How did it happen?'

I moved off the front porch.

'Look, Bob and I can help. When Bob gets home from work, we'll start looking in the park.'

She began to yell, 'Chewy, Chewy, Chewy,' and then walked up the front steps into her house.

'Thanks, Patty,' I yelled too late.

Then I realised I'd forgotten to take Chewy's leash.

Great, I thought, another bonehead move. I went back inside to get Chewy's leash. *Time to get serious*, I thought, *Time to stop fooling around.*

* * *

Chewy wasn't fooling around. He ran down the canal embankment and over to the park for the cool shade of the leafy trees, sniffing their splotching grey-ridged bark. Chewy was in dog heaven again – here were his old stomping grounds with no leash on and no humans jerking him around. In the park he could sniff when and where he wanted. For him, sniffing splashed-urine scattered trees, old posts and telegraph poles was like reading *The New York Times*: catching up on current events, discovering who was in heat and when, and noting what dog marked where. Illumination, wonder, astonishment, information...

For Chewy escape was a great adventure: roaming where he wanted, when he wanted, and the way he wanted. He could stop, or zig-zag across streets; he could greet strange new people and go up to them and smell their outstretched fingers. You'd be amazed at what smells are on people's hands and under their finger-nails – salmon oils from lunch, garlic stains from pizza. And best of all, those meat smells. It was a dog's heaven. Some people even let you lick their fingers.

Or he could sniff the freshly cut park grass for yummy morsels such as droppings from Big Macs oozing with mayonnaise and onions and every once in a while Chicken McNuggets covered in dirt. He could swim in the canal, or drink from it; snap at bugs, play with other dogs and explore new alleys and streets. Or he could go down people's sidewalks, or sniff along the sides of houses into their backyards. He could eat cat food that was left outside, pull open garbage bags, stick his head through fences or snarl at fenced-in dogs. Even laugh at cats or chase them, if he wanted. Hundreds of things he couldn't do with a human at the other end of a leash. What a great adventure!

Chapter Seventeen
Our Worst Nightmare

For Lauren and me Chewy's great adventure was a nightmare.

Lauren kept trying to focus on her work. She tried to stay focused at the meeting but every few minutes a delicate little thought of Chewy would disrupt her like a secret frightened bark from him to just her.

After the meeting, she found herself sitting in her chair staring out the window, clearing her throat and strumming her fingers on the edges of her desk. She puzzled as to why she could barely understand a recent piece of legislation she was reviewing. A single word would stop her and then suddenly she would imagine herself walking down the alley behind our house looking everywhere for her beloved pup.

By the time Lauren came home, I had walked the immediate neighbourhood shouting: 'Chewy, Chewy, Chewy.' I shouted it loudly; I called softly. I shouted it down tree-lined streets and while walking through neighbourhood alleys. I knew I looked ridiculous. I knew neighbours who didn't know me saw a sixty-five-year-old balding man in tennis shoes, paint-splashed jeans and a T-shirt with a faded logo walking back and forth across the street, shouting something they couldn't quite make out. My hair was beaten by the wind; my prune face obviously in pain. *Who knew where I had come from*, they must have thought. Maybe I had escaped from the state hospital. Babbling like crazy, something about a dog. Was I sane? Perhaps I was just homeless, coming off as a drunk. Maybe I was demented, or temporally delusional. But who knew, and more importantly, who wanted to find out?

Some closed their doors. Most others yelled out, 'What's up? What's going on? A kidnapping? Somebody take your daughter?'

'No, no, no,' I yelled through cupped hands, standing on the front lawn of their duplex apartment. 'It's only my dog. He got out.'

Only my dog, I thought. Lucky Lauren didn't hear that. *Only my stupid mistake*. I thanked them for asking and went home to wait for Lauren.

When Lauren clicked open the front door, she heard me in the shower. The hot water pinpricked the tension out of my shoulder muscles. My head hung forward, relaxed. All worry about Chewy was gone. Warm water dribbled down my forehead, circled to my nose and dripped off in a constant wobbly stream.

'Will you be ready soon?' Lauren asked, poking her head into the bathroom steam.

'Give me a minute,' I responded.

After I had dried off and changed clothes, I explained to Lauren that I'd been walking the streets looking for Chewy. No luck. She was distraught. We agreed that I should stay home in the event Chewy came back. Since I had already searched the near neighbourhood, Lauren decided to drive around to Chewy's old haunts to see if she could find him. Besides, she felt the need to act: she needed to find him and bring him home.

In the driveway, she opened her car window, leaned her head out and kissed me goodbye. 'Wish me luck!'

'After I look, I'm going straight back to work,' she added, her eyebrows knotted, 'I'm really worried – we could lose him.'

Lauren promised to be back at 5 p.m. directly after work, her words trying to hide the worry in her voice.

'We'll find him,' I said. 'I'm sure we will.'

But I wasn't sure of anything, let alone finding Chewy again. I looked up at the grey barked sycamore tree before our house, its branches spun out to catch sunlight. *We have to find him*, I thought. *I'll never forgive myself if we don't.*

Lauren drove over to Gary's house, parked and walked a short way up along the canal, looking for Chewy in the bushes and fences. Children playing at the canal bridge watched her. Their mother sat in the park on the grass and watched her. Lauren walked past the children and said, 'Hello,' thinking, *I'm not a very good mother to Chewy. You've got a good mother.*

Then she drove up Virginia Avenue with her window rolled down, looking for Chewy. *He could hide anywhere*, she thought, looking in the swaying tendrils, behind the twined ivy stitched up the fences and tree bark. Nothing. Nothing behind or under the oleander bushes; nothing behind the park benches along the bike trail either. When two women rode down the bike trail on shiny new pink bicycles Lauren thought of asking them if they had seen a dog. *Oh, this isn't helping*, she thought. She turned down Roseburg Avenue, a street where neighbours had previously told her they'd often seen Chewy.

Glancing up driveways, Lauren saw nothing. How can a big dog disappear? Just disappear? She drove over to College Avenue, another one of Chewy's favourite places. On College Avenue all she saw were college students clustered at a bus stop, or strolling across campus to classes.

She circled back and drove back down College Avenue. Nothing. Then cut over to Tully Avenue, cruising through middle-class neighbourhoods. No luck anywhere. Just empty streets. No glimpse of him. No tail turning down an alley. No bark. Nothing.

She even drove over to 9th Street, driving up and down the downtown area to where 9th Street ended. Her friend Deirdre had told her she had seen Chewy roaming around 9th Street a few times prior to us getting him off the streets. No luck once again. Where was he?

After an hour driving through a tangle of streets, frustration and failure squeezed out Lauren's hope and she gave up. She could not reasonably be gone from work any longer. Her fingers tightened their grip on the steering wheel. Hungry and defeated, she drove back into the parking garage at work. Depressed, she thought, *if we lose him I'm going to be so upset. All that effort and worry...*

Riding up the elevator to her office, Lauren had a bright idea. Once she got back to the office, she called Cecelia. She left Cecelia a message on her answering machine at home. She told Cecelia the whole sad story as if she was talking to a priest in a confession. Lauren described how panicked she was, how little luck they'd had so far; how hopeless it seemed. She added that she hoped Cecelia could find the time to help: she knew Cecelia would be tired after work but Chewy needed help. She also knew Cecelia *would* help. They needed to find Chewy so he didn't get hurt. 'We're the only family he's got,' she added, and then hung up.

Of course, the minute Cecelia got home at 4.30 p.m. and heard the message, she got back into her car, still in her nurse's outfit, and drove towards the canal and the parks. Her eyes were everywhere: on plants, behind garbage bags, under bushes around corners, in stairwells, squinting under cars looking for Chewy but no luck.

Block after block of no luck...

Then she heard the shouts: 'Chewy, Chewy, Chewy!' The shouts sounded like football chants from the Chewy rescue team coming from the Modesto Junior College stadium, four blocks away.

'Chewy, Chewy, Chewy!'

Two men walking down the sidewalk a few feet in front of her car heard the chants also. They stopped and looked up at the trees. One elbowed the other. Then Cecelia slowly drove past, looking like she was going to ask for directions.

'Lady, you need help?' one of the men asked as she cruised by.

Cecelia didn't know what to do but she pressed the button to automatically lower the car window nearest the kerb, then leaned across the seat and said, 'Have you seen a big red furry dog – a Saint Bernard/Collie mix running loose? Did he go by here?'

'A *what*?' they responded.

'A dog, a big furry red dog – a Saint Bernard/Collie mix! Oh, he's so lovely! You'd know him if you saw him, he's beautiful. His beauty would stand out if you saw him.'

Cecelia was now wishing she hadn't bothered to ask them. It felt hopeless.

'Yeah, we saw him,' the short one said, 'a big red guy running fast. He went over that way towards the park.' He pointed to Graceada Park.

'He ran right through traffic and almost got wacked,' the taller one added. 'Hope that helps,' he said, smiling.

Cecelia thanked them profusely.

'Is that what all the yelling is about?'

'I think so,' Cecelia said.

'Well, if it is, you better get going. He ran by here twenty minutes ago, lickedy split, like he was gonna catch a train. He knew where he was going; he was on a mission. He disappeared down the block.'

The skinny arm of the tall man rose up and pointed across the street again towards the park.

'He was cuttin', he was gunning it.'

Then they heard, 'Chewy, Chewy, Chewy,' again through the trees.

'Thank you,' Cecelia said to the two men.

She drove off fast, intent on finding Chewy before anything happened to him. If Cecelia had any luck left, she hoped it would be here for her this time. So far no one else had had any.

* * *

Not me, sitting on the front porch swing, waiting. Over the roof of Bob and Patty's house, I heard the shouts for Chewy. From down the block towards Gracaeda Park, Denise, who had been out walking Boss, had heard Lauren shouting. She'd joined Patty and Bob.

The whole neighbourhood was alive with shouts. I stood up; I could not sit in the front porch swing, waiting for Chewy to turn up any more. My right leg was bouncing up and down like a jackhammer, begging me to move. I frowned and grew angry with myself. *What a bonehead move*, I thought, *all this work trying to get Chewy off the streets gone in one stupid mistake.* It's not like I had noticed Chewy squint-eyed and calculating his escape. Hell, he hadn't even been close to the screen door. Chewy was quick, though, and determined; his body had slammed against my leg and had almost knocked me down. It was a block the NFL would have loved.

I had to do something, not just sit here. Chewy had been gone most of the day. I decided to get a leash, some dog cookie treats for Chewy should I find him, a bag for poop and my keys. I then locked the front door, cut across the driveway and our neighbours' front lawn, turned left and walked back down the sidewalk into the alley. At least I could check out the alley again. Perhaps Chewy was hiding back in the alley, frightened and lonely.

Of course the alley was empty. Only Mr Sivero's van with Sivero Plumbing painted on the side, the 'P' for Plumbing painted out by someone, was there. A couple of squashed grapefruits were on the ground where Denise and Rob's tree hung its branches over their high side fence. Mr Sivero's garbage bins were kicked over, empty and foul-smelling as I walked by. I set the bins upright.

'Chewieeeee, Chewieeeee,' I called, desperation turning to frustration. Halfway down the alley I could see there was no Chewy in sight. I'd know if he was in the alley; the house at the end of the alley with six dogs would have been a howling, yelping mess by now. Chester, the big German Shepherd with bad hips, would be screeching like a wolf. Also, the little dogs would have been yapping and running back and forth along the back fence, chasing ghosts. Probably the chickens in their backyard would have hopped the fence and come squawking and flapping their clipped wings down the alley at me. I couldn't hear anyone yelling 'Chewy, Chewy!' Perhaps Denise or Lauren had found him? Maybe Bob and Patty had discovered him hiding in some bushes? I hoped so. Somebody had to get lucky.

I walked out of the alley back onto Magnolia Avenue, heading home. The earlier plan of me staying home in case Chewy made it back made sense, I thought. In the meantime, Lauren, Patty and Bob had split up, heading down different streets but in the same general direction, south and towards the parks. Lauren walked down the length of Elmwood Avenue four blocks but Chewy was nowhere to be seen. Cecelia, unbeknownst to Lauren, drove west along West Morris Avenue. After talking to the two men, she turned south, driving along the far side of the parks. Bob and Patty headed towards Graceada Park. Denise, with Boss in tow, cut across Magnolia Avenue towards the parks. I sat on the front porch.

The hunt was now on in full force – a combined neighbourhood effort.

'Chewy, Chewy, Chewy!' All were walking the neighbourhood, calling 'Chewy, Chewy, where are you? Chewy, it's time to come home. Where are you, you silly boy?' On Magnolia Avenue, a light blue Chevy with a fifty-five-year-old man in a moussed-up crew cut pulled up in front of the house. I sat on the front porch, waiting; I liked the car.

'What's going on?' the man asked, 'Is somebody missing? Need any help?'

I stood up and walked over to his chopped and channelled car. 'Nice car,' I smiled. This is what I love about Modesto: people are still willing to help.

The man had a US Marine motto 'Semper Fidelis' (Always Faithful) tattoo on his arm, hanging out the window.

'Nah, we're OK. Just lost our dog – we'll find him, for sure. Thank you for offering to help.'

'Sure you will,' the guy said, 'just checking.' He revved his engine and took off driving towards Elmwood Avenue. It sounded like his mufflers were dragging.

Two blocks down Elmwood Avenue Lauren turned towards Graceada Park. When she walked one block back to Magnolia Avenue, Bob saw her.

'Lauren, Lauren, we've been looking for you!' he shouted, his breath amplifying his voice like a megaphone. He raised his arms above his head, waving like a policeman trying to stop a car.

'Come quickly, they found him!' Bob pivoted and pointed at the tennis courts. 'Chewy's at the park! He's on the other side of the tennis courts, just lying on the grass. We need to get over there pronto before he takes off again.'

Lauren was stunned. Chewy was in the park! Relief poured through her. She started running the remaining three blocks to the tennis courts. After two blocks, her thighs felt like cement but still she ran, trembling with excitement. *Chewy, my God, they found Chewy*! Whatever else she'd wished for in her life she wished for this one simple wish: let Chewy be there. Let Chewy be there sitting on the grass in the sunlight.

When she reached Bob, he explained that Denise and Patty were headed into the park to try and steer him back towards Lauren's house. Lauren took a deep breath and told herself to calm down – this was no time to go ballistic, Chewy needed a calm presence. She and Bob caught up with Denise and Patty then the four of them headed towards the tennis courts.

When Lauren saw Boss, she smiled and said, 'Oh, I'm so glad Boss is here too! He should be able to reassure Chewy.'

When they got to the park, Lauren blinked: there was Chewy. Even from this distance she could see he was panting heavily and he was jumpy. His head was jerking back and forth in short little movements; he looked exhausted. He looked right through Lauren as she walked towards him. Seeing Lauren and Bob, he started backing up.

Lauren stopped and sat down on the grass on the opposite end of the tennis courts. Denise came up beside her with Boss. Bob and Patty waited behind them.

'Oh, he looks beat up and exhausted,' Denise said. The wind sputtered through the trees.

'He looks really tired,' Lauren said. Watching Chewy swaying on his haunches, obviously frightened and overwhelmed, she intertwined her fingers and squeezed them together. *Now let's take this slowly*, she thought.

First, this is good, she told herself. *He had his run in the streets, his escape, but now he's ready to come home. He's stressed out and frightened. Escape isn't fun anymore. We will just have to bring him home safely. Be gentle and patient, girl.* Lauren suddenly thought of the comment Cecelia's sister Charlotte had made the night Chewy was drugged: 'Sure is a lot of effort for one dog.' Here they were again, trying to bring this dog home.

As Denise, Boss and Lauren walked closer to Chewy, he backed up. *How do we reassure him?* Lauren puzzled.

Denise said, 'Let's sit down and see if he'll come over to us. He'll probably come for Boss, if nothing else.'

They sat down in the short grass between two trees and started talking as if nothing in the world mattered except having a casual good time relaxing in the shade and sunlight, talking and laughing.

Chewy noticed them. He turned his head, his eyes catching Lauren and unbelievably, like a little lost lemming, he started trotting over towards them. His white mane was bouncing in the wind as he increased his tempo to reach them. As he got closer, he stopped by the trees close to Lauren and Denise. Boss watching, Chewy wondering why his friend was hesitant to come over and play. Lauren's heart was soaring. She could feel her neck muscles squeeze tight. As Chewy came closer she pushed her palms down into the grass. With every step of his white paws, Lauren had to fight the urge to shout out his name and reach for his lovely, big old body. Oh, this was driving her nuts!

'Chewy!' burst out of her mouth like a grenade exploding. It startled him.

He stopped five feet from her. Chewy stopped and looked at her and then lay down in the grass, turning his head away when he heard someone walking behind him.

Lauren closed her eyes. *You're an idiot*, she thought. She exhaled deeply and said to Denise, 'Let's just sit here for a moment and then I'm going to try to put a leash on him. Maybe he'll let me. Thank goodness Boss is here to help.'

Boss sat on the grass next to Denise. When he saw Chewy, he started to whine and to get up. Denise restrained him. Chewy saw what was happening. He looked at Lauren and Denise, and then sank down into the grass, clearly focused on Boss. Patty and Bob continued to hang back in the shadows.

Chewy crawled closer to Lauren.

Oh, good, Lauren thought. *This is a good sign.* She was also pleased to see his collar was still on. Reaching over to him to attach the leash, he shied off. *Here we go again*, she thought, *just like months ago at the canal bridge.* Her fingers reached out a second and third time. Each time Chewy ducked the leash but came forward again. *He wants to come home*, Lauren thought, but each time she reached out with the leash in her hand, Chewy's head sunk back down, slipping beneath her fingers just out of reach.

Kneeling on the grass Lauren was confused and frustrated. Clearly he was scared – but why? He'd been on this very leash for weeks whenever Lauren took him on walks. She let her hand holding the leash drop to her side. Why was he still so scared?

Out of the corner of her eye Lauren saw Cecelia watching this strange dance between herself and Chewy. Cecelia had parked her car some twenty feet from Lauren and Denise. With her window down she silently watched the events unfold. Lauren brightened. With Cecelia there, she felt herself relax. She closed her eyes again and took a deep breath. *Everything will be OK*, she told herself. Her shoulders dropped as the panic left with each new breath.

Then Bob's foot dangled down beside her. Patty and Bob came up behind Denise and Lauren and then sat down.

'Any good ideas?' Lauren asked Patty.

'I think we should just go,' Denise said.

'You think we should just go?' Patty repeated. 'How will that help?' She looked at Bob. He shrugged his shoulders and threw up his hands.

'I don't mean just go,' Denise said.

Lauren looked perplexed.

'Look,' Denise said. 'Nothing has worked so far. He's freaked out and tired. Boss is the draw, I think. Maybe if we all just stood up and slowly walked back to Lauren's house Chewy might follow, especially since Boss is here.'

'Why don't you let Boss off-leash? Maybe he'll go over to Chewy and calm him down' Lauren suggested.

'You think?' Bob responded.

'It's worth a try,' said Patty.

Denise unclipped the leash from Boss's collar. Untied, the black hump of his shoulders rose up like a submarine out of a sea of grass and in a series of quick leaps he stood beside Chewy, who rose up to greet him. Both dogs engaged in the customary dog greeting of sniffing each other. Lauren and Denise thought the dogs would start playing. For a second, Lauren thought, *Oh my God, what if they both take off?* She could see them disappearing across the park, playing with each other.

Unexpectedly, Boss's paws folded, his rump dropped to the earth. Boss's black fur melted onto the grass. Chewy collapsed beside him. Both dogs sat quietly looking around.

'Well, so much for that,' Lauren said.

'Why don't we just get up and walk back to your house?' suggested Denise. She motioned to Boss, who came over and allowed himself to be leashed. Chewy's eyes followed what was happening.

Lauren looked at Denise quizzically. 'Really?'

Denise nodded; Bob and Patty simply shrugged their shoulders.

'Why not?' Patty said.

The more Lauren thought about it, the more she realised it might work if only because Boss was with them: Chewy might just follow Boss. *Denise and Boss could just come right into our house*, she thought. She got up.

They all got up. Lauren yelled over to Cecelia their new plan. Cecelia smiled and nodded back 'yes'. Boss touched his shoulders against Denise's thigh getting up, turned around and looked at Chewy.

Boss barked. In this last moment, whatever dog communication was in that bark and in Boss's tail, swinging like a metro dome, Chewy wasted no time tightening his leg and chest muscles to push himself up. He then shook himself off and trotted over towards the group walking away. Lauren's eyebrows rose; she was smiling at Denise. Denise mouthed silently, 'I told you so', and off they went. Now it was six of them, with Chewy trailing behind.

Lauren acted casually, not looking to see if Chewy was still behind them. Three blocks home seemed like 3,000 miles. After a block she couldn't control herself and looked round. Surprisingly Chewy had not only followed them but came right up to the walking legs and swinging arms, and slipped in between Boss and Lauren. Lauren felt Chewy bump her thigh.

Denise and Lauren grinned at each other.

Lauren raised her right hand, looked sideways down at Chewy walking beside her. She looked at Denise. With her left index finger she stabbed her finger into her right hand repeatedly. Her eyes caught Denise's, her lips mouthing, 'I don't believe it, I don't believe it!' To herself she thought, *This is perfect, this is perfect*!

After the second block and in view of her house, Lauren could no longer feel her feet touching the ground. She was floating on air, holding her breath, elated, wanting to scream 'Yes, yes!' but too scared to do anything but put one foot in front of the other and nonchalantly stroll on home.

Stroll on home they did. *Holy moly*, Lauren thought, *I will be walking up the front steps of our home with Chewy by my side*! And they did just that.

When the group reached our house, Lauren walked up the front porch and opened the front door with Chewy beside her, anxious to get in. Without pausing, without looking back at Boss and Denise, Chewy walked right in, no problem. He was relieved to be home.

When his tail disappeared inside, Lauren thought, *No problem, no problem. Amazing*! She pulled the front door shut and let the screen door shut slowly. Everybody clapped. Lauren gave Boss a big sloppy hug and thanked Denise.

'What a deal!' Lauren said, and thanked everybody again and again. Bob and Patty walked across the street and into their house. Denise and Lauren hugged, and then Denise started walking Boss home.

'Amazing, isn't it?' Lauren said. 'Thanks again.'

She waved goodbye to Denise, who was down the block at that point. *What a friend*, Lauren thought. Then Lauren noticed Cecelia. She had followed them in her car and had parked near the house. Lauren walked over and talked to her through the open car door window.

'I'm so relieved. I was not certain Chewy would make it back to our house – I thought we might have to start all over again,' Lauren said.

'He's an angel,' Cecelia said. 'What a relief!'

Lauren thanked Cecelia for her help and told her how glad she was that Cecelia was there. Somehow, having Cecelia watching the events in the park provided assurance for Lauren. Maybe Cecelia was the true angel, not Chewy.

After Cecelia left to drive home, Lauren walked back up the front steps to where I was waiting inside. I'd noticed the group walking down the streets while hovering near the front door. Seeing Chewy, I'd quickly gone indoors, not wanting to spook him.

When Lauren entered the house, Chewy was crashed out on the floor. He was exhausted from his day's adventure. Lauren and I went into the kitchen, talking about what had happened.

Hearing our voices, Chewy came into the kitchen too. Lauren knew Chewy must be hungry after his day's adventure, so she gave him some of his favourite treats:

chicken chews and wet dog food. She and I watched Chewy with his muzzle buried in his food. The bowl of food emptied in a blizzard of scraping incisors and tongue lickings.

Leaning against the kitchen counter, I said, 'I think he was trying to make it back home. I think he might not have been able to figure out how to get back home.'

'I agree,' Lauren said. Then she realised the clinking sound of Chewy's collar and ID tags hitting the bowl were missing. She looked around and Chewy was gone.

Lauren and I walked round the house until we got to the bedroom. Chewy was sound asleep on his big, thick comfy bed. Lauren looked at him, thinking, *I hope you've learned your lesson today, Mr Chewy. It's exhausting being out in the streets, isn't it, Chewy boy? I'm glad you're home, Chewy!*

The great escape was over in a flash – the first great escape. I couldn't believe my eyes: all that work, all that anxiety. All that drama, and there we were in the bedroom, watching Chewy's paws jiggle and contract as he chased something in his dreams. Breathing slowly and safely on his dog bed, he was safe at last.

'What now?' Lauren asked.

'I don't know,' I quipped.

'How about homemade pizza and a movie?'

Chapter Eighteen
Is Chewy Transforming?

'Look at him,' Lauren whispered from her chair. She reached over and touched my arm.

I was emotionally exhausted; spaced out, watching *Transformers Two*, I was hoping Bumblebee's wounds would heal. After roughly six hours of terror I needed a little mindless fantasy; so did Lauren. Chewy was back, asleep at my feet. Lauren had collapsed into her favourite chair, a stack of unread mail and bills to pay on her lap. Watching a movie made doing paperwork easier. My feet were propped up on the couch.

'Look at him,' she said nodding her head in Chewy's direction, 'he's crashed out. Acting like nothing had happened.'

'Snoring?' I said. 'He can't be snoring?'

Part of me was outraged. His paws were jiggling and every once in a while a little shudder went through his body. He was on his side, front legs slightly bent, eyes closed, mouth opened. *All the energy, all the drama of the last six hours, and he comes home and goes to sleep. Give me a break!*

I watched him breathing; saw the curly hairs on his belly, the thin white fur that stuck out between his paw toes as he kneaded in his sleep. After all, he was exhausted, too. He had been excruciatingly frightened. And he didn't ask to be our dog – he was our responsibility, in our care. We were supposed to feed and protect him. Suddenly I realised how self-centred I was in being outraged. I couldn't deny I felt it but I didn't have to do anything except notice it. The most important things were Chewy's safety, getting him back and how wonderfully our neighbours had rallied round not only to save him but to help us bring him back to his home.

Lauren tapped my arm again, and looked over at me – 'He's pretty wonderful, isn't he?'

I knew she was right.

While I was enjoying this tender little moment, Chewy farted. Astounded, my jaw dropped. The mood was gone – I didn't know dogs could fart.

'Keeping it real,' Lauren said, smiling.

* * *

The next day Chewy was the same old Chewy. He acted as if nothing had happened. And perhaps from his dog's perspective nothing had. He was simply out for a run, a prolonged stroll, got frightened and exhausted. Maybe he discovered the streets weren't as free and easy as he remembered. Being on the streets for a day he might have been reminded just how scary and difficult being homeless was. Perhaps even he was trying to come home when he heard all the shouting and commotion. *Humans*, he may have thought, *humans make mountains out of molehills.*

'After all, walking with my friend Boss,' he might say, 'I came right back and sauntered into the house, no problem. What else do you want? If you hadn't gone ballistic, I would have been back on your front porch in a half-hour or so. Lighten up, have a little faith.'

Who knows what the truth of his great escape was?

Over the next few days and weeks he still sometimes refused to come in at night. He was still finicky about his food; he did not just eat anything that was given him. Lauren always made sure he was given healthier types of dog food plus a few treats. You would think since Chewy had been a stray and underweight living on the streets he would gobble down his food. Not Chewy; he was particular. And if you raised your voice too loud, or were visibly upset, he became extremely frightened, skittish.

All of this may simply have been a normal part of adapting to the changes in his life. Our hope for a quick bonding with us seemed illusory; we couldn't expect to win his trust easily, we would have to earn it.

Several days later, Lauren called me while I was in my studio.

'Come, look at this,' she said. I put down my big brush and walked outside. Lauren was standing at the bottom of the back step, leash in hand. She let out a sigh.

'Look at this,' she repeated.

As I passed the edge of the studio, I saw what she meant.

Chewy was pacing back and forth on the pathway at the end of the garden near the back fence. He'd glance up, pace, glance down and up again as if he expected to be set upon.

'He looks upset,' I said. 'What's going on?' At the sound of my voice Chewy stopped and looked over at me.

'Oh, I can't even get this leash on him to go for something he wants – his afternoon walk. Got any ideas?'

I looked over at her.

'I'm on a mission,' she insisted.

You don't want to get in between Lauren and one of her missions. She's like a momma bear and her cub; she'd fight to the death for her mission. So I wished her luck, told her I had no ideas any better than hers and I knew she'd figure it out. I retreated back into my studio to paint.

Half an hour and several frustrated mutterings later, Lauren stuck her head through my studio door.

'Look.'

I looked. Chewy's head was sticking through the white curtains framing the studio door, right below Lauren's head. She was smiling; I wasn't so sure about Chewy.

'How did you do that?' I asked.

'It's a girl thing,' she said.

'Yeah, right,' I said, 'A girl thing!'

'I'll tell you later,' she said, laughing.

* * *

An hour later, when the back door opened, Chewy came running down the steps onto the sidewalk. This time he was smiling. I went outside to learn about this 'girl thing'; I was pretty sure Lauren may have discovered something but it wasn't a girl thing – whatever that meant.

'OK, OK,' I said to Lauren, 'show me your secret.'

Here's what she said: 'I got tired of walking around the backyard, chasing him. The minute he's not sure what you want, he gets scared. When he behaves like this it's best just to go sit on the back steps and call to him. Given time, he will eventually walk over to you. Once he's near you on the back steps if you rub and pet him while talking softly to him – telling him he's a good boy, and handsome, a special doggie – he will respond. It doesn't matter what you say but you have to use gentle tones. Today, after a while talking to him like this, I was able to put the leash on him. I was then able to lead him into the house and then we could go for a walk. What is so silly about all of this is I know he loves having his walks: it's the highlight of his day.'

She sighed. 'Tonight, I'll sit on the back porch and talk to him to try to coax him into the house. I want him to come inside at least periodically. He doesn't have to come in every night like Emma, but I want a dog that will stay with you. Maybe he has to learn that; maybe he needs to feel safe in the house. I want Chewy inside the house at night, sleeping on his dog bed in our bedroom.'

Lauren raised her eyebrows, her eyes widened. She tightened her lips and her cheeks puffed out, then she gave me a look that said, am I being unreasonable about this?

Chewy, as a stray, knew living outside. Now he had to learn to like staying inside. It made sense. His big fluffy doggie bed helped, provided the cats weren't sleeping on it. So, I started lifting them off whenever Chewy came into the bedroom. I made a big deal about it.

The cats curled up in a bundle on Chewy's bed didn't flick their tails, yawn or move a muscle. They appeared to be oblivious to what was in store for them: a disruption to their peaceful napping. It didn't matter that they had nice fluffy cat beds of their own – they preferred Chewy's bed.

'Oh,' I said with fake outrage, 'look at this, Mr Chewy.' I would sweep open my arms above the bed and the cats. 'Look at this, Mr Chewy, they're on YOUR bed! Well, we'll fix that.' I shot a glance at Chewy, peeking around the end of our bed, just his muzzle and eyes showing, and then, addressing each cat individually as Mr Leo or Ms Gracie, I lifted them ceremoniously off Chewy's bed and onto ours. Sometimes the cats, knowing they were guilty or simply scared by my arm gestures, fled on their own. When all the cats were removed, I turned, bowed to Chewy as if he were royalty and with a grand gesture of my left hand, invited him to step onto his doggie bed.

I know my behaviour sounds crazy and I only have the faintest glimmer of hope that my actions made Chewy feel welcome or protected in some way. Possibly, all it did was confuse him more profoundly. Perhaps the change the behaviour induced wasn't in Chewy but in me.

I don't know.

* * *

What it did do was lead me to notice other ways the cats were giving Chewy a hard time. One evening, I noticed how Fred was, I think purposefully, I won't say bullying Chewy but at least making life harder for him. And so I intervened on Chewy's behalf. With my behaviour, I'm sure Chewy felt protected, possibly he even appreciated it; it definitely made coming in at night easier for him and I think it helped him bond with us.

Fred, his whiteness, was on the steps, staring up at me. Chewy lay three feet behind him on the back-yard sidewalk, his paws forwards, head turned slightly right and resting on his paws. There was no eye contact between the two. A swishing white tail signalled Fred's intent: 'I'm angry, don't mess with me, dude.'

I didn't know what was up between them. Lauren had called Chewy; I was checking to see what had held him up.

Fred held him up; he held him up purposefully. Who knew why? Chewy had been a perfect gentlemen, at least when Lauren or I'd seen him interacting with Fred.

Is Chewy Transforming?

I'm not much good at reading dog or cat as a second language. It's a fact that I barely made it through French in college, using interlinear translations and hiding behind a huge football linebacker in French class so the teacher didn't see me praying I wouldn't get called upon. Besides, English is a tough enough language for me as it is.

'Fred,' I whispered, 'do you mind moving so Chewy can get by?'

It was risky to pick Fred up when he was in one of his moods. He did not put up with being handled if he did not approve; you might just get scratched. After all, who was in charge here. Fred? You betcha!

'Fred, why don't you let Chewy by?'

No response.

So a little more than gently, I pushed my toe under Fred's behind. He swatted, looked up at me and slowly walked into the kitchen. His haunches were high, almost regal, and each step was a statement of defiance, his tail switching for punctuation.

Chewy saw the whole drama. He looked up at me as soon as Fred disappeared into the kitchen, shook himself off like he was waking from a bad dream, jumped up the back steps and sauntered into the kitchen for dinner. This became a routine and sometimes Chewy nudged me with his nose on my leg just before going into the kitchen, like he was saying, 'Thanks, Dad. Fred can be such a pain in the ass!'

I couldn't have agreed more.

Slowly, the boundaries with Fred changed, and in my mind at least, Chewy and I were learning to trust each other. I say this because sometimes Chewy came up close to me and nudged me when Fred was blocking his exit into the backyard. This I took as a sign that Chewy was saying, 'There he goes again, can you move him for me, please?' When I moved Fred, Chewy bound down the back steps into the backyard like a gazelle. It seemed to me I was training him and he was training me.

Yet, in spite of this Chewy still refused to come in several nights of the week. Also, his eating was even more uneven: some nights he ate, others he didn't. Sometimes he just picked at his food, and some nights he just looked at the food with what I can only describe as contempt, or perhaps distain.

He stared into his dog bowl, did a little double take, sniffed it, sometimes lolled his tongue down to lick some morsel, or perhaps what he hoped was a morsel, and then abruptly turned first his head and then his whole body away. *Oh, please*, he seemed to be saying, *you can do a whole lot better than this!*

It wasn't that Lauren fed him, or our cats for that matter, boring or bland run-of-the-mill food. Their diet included organic chicken or beef jerky, two or three different kinds of wet food with vegetables, dry food and several varieties of doggie treats. When it came to doggie treats Chewy showed his like or dislike by eating them up or leaving them in his bowl for some other critter. By trial and error, Lauren did a considerable amount of research as to what to feed Chewy.

Yet Chewy remained finicky and reserved about his eating. I couldn't figure him out.

As a stray he was 20–25 per cent underweight. Obviously, scrounging for food had left him underweight but not seriously malnourished. His coat was thick, his teeth full of plaque but not diseased, his gums and eyes fine and his muscle tone appropriate. And most importantly, his blood work was normal.

Living with us, he quickly gained weight, so clearly he was eating something. But since his breakfast bowl was typically placed before the French doors to my studio, I routinely observed what he ate and didn't eat, and many days he didn't eat anything or very little. He might have been acting in response to being rescued. Perhaps he was merely frightened and depressed. Maybe his eating habits were those of a 'grazer', consuming small portions several times a day. Soldiers develop Post Traumatic Stress Disorder in response to extreme stress; maybe Chewy was suffering from a doggie's Post Traumatic Rescue Disorder. After all he'd been abducted and drugged, operated upon, lived in three homes in five weeks and now he was living with two fierce cats, all in a short period of time, a matter of months.

How did his new home compare with living on the street as a stray? I didn't know. On the one hand he'd voluntarily come back from his first great escape. Obviously, escape was stressful. Lauren and I didn't trust Chewy off-leash or for him to sit in the front yard while Lauren gardened. Given the chance, we felt Chewy would run.

We didn't trust him – and Chewy didn't trust us. He was wary of his food; often he refused his leash. Given the opportunity, he'd run . He didn't want to come in at night; he was bored out of his mind during the day. And Fred and Pip had bullied him on his first day.

Night after night, I heard the same old refrain: 'He won't come in to eat.'

'He won't come in, again,' Lauren said to me one night. As usual, she was standing by the back door. 'I want him to come in and be with us – this is frustrating.'

Chewy, a few feet down the sidewalk before the door, simply looked up at her. His rear end was in darkness – it was like the darkness was enveloping him. Like he was slipping over to the dark side of fear or stubbornness, or some kind of street sense we didn't understand, or maybe something else entirely. We were disappointed. Looking out the kitchen window, I didn't know what to do.

'I've had it!' Lauren declared, impatience and defeat in her voice. She came in the kitchen, handed me Chewy's bowl and said, 'See if you can get him in. If he won't come in, I've had it with him. He can stay out all night, see if I care! If he doesn't come in, he doesn't get dinner.'

I could tell Lauren felt hopeless as to how to bond further with Chewy. For that matter, so did I.

Is Chewy Transforming?

Well, when Lauren talks like that, I've learned to get out of the way (I suspected Chewy was about to learn that too). I went outside and tried to butter him up. Sitting on the porch three feet from him, I talked to him. I'm a tough-minded empiricist: just show me the evidence, the empirical data. However, when it came to Chewy, I was slipping over to the dark side: shameless anthropomorphising with him, calling him my little friend, my buddy, explaining the intricacies of what Lauren wanted like I was talking to an English Literature graduate student at U.C. Berkeley, instead of a dog who I believed had the cognitive capacity of a young child. Except with me there was that part of me that also knew – even if I couldn't verbalise it – that there was something more: I'd seen it in Chewy's eyes.

And so I explained to Chewy what Lauren wanted: for him to come in and eat dinner with us, be a dog at her feet while we watched movies or read. More than likely the pleading and gentle softness of my tone softened Chewy. He sat in front of me, letting me stroke his head, peacefully. For a moment or two, I thought I was Cesar Millan, the dog whisperer.

The backyard was completely dark; the porch light silhouetted Chewy and I. Moths were fluttering around the porch light. I decided to go inside the house, hoping Chewy would follow.

Wrong.

He watched me go in. When I closed the back door and looked out the small-framed window in the back door, he gazed up at me quizzically. Then he turned right and walked into the bushes by the air-conditioning unit. He walked over into the dark side of the yard.

About 3 a.m., flashlight in hand, I checked on him: he was snuggled asleep in his shallow observation hole. He was still there asleep at 7.30 a.m. when I put his morning food bowl out in front of my studio. He didn't come over to eat.

'I knew it,' Lauren said. 'We're going to have a contest of wills.'

Chewy doesn't know it, but he's picked the wrong woman to mess with, I thought.

That evening he didn't eat.

I know that a behaviourist could analyse our series of interactions with Chewy and probably point out how we had subtly reinforced and created this situation for ourselves, but the reality is that after a long seven-day stand-off, Chewy started coming in for dinner on a regular basis. Also, staying for movies and sleeping in the bedroom on his bed.

Bonding seemed to require setting some firm limits, consistently applied. Lauren provided these. It may be that in Chewy's mind she was established as the alpha dog. After all, she took him on most of his walks and she fed him each day. She gardened in his backyard; she held conversations with him on a regular basis.

Is Chewy Transforming?

At this point, Lauren spent the most time with Chewy and I was something of an afterthought. But that was about to change.

Chapter Nineteen
Another Try at Training

'It's time,' Lauren said.

'I'm ready,' I responded.

'I'm talking about Chewy,' she went on. 'He barked this afternoon.'

She got up from weeding the garden and walked over to me. It was Sunday afternoon. Three artist friends were coming over for a drawing session. I had been cleaning my studio, arranging chairs and drawing tables. My friends were due to arrive in half an hour.

'What do you mean, he barked?'

'You know, woof, woof, woof.' She looked at me like I was brain dead. 'He barked just like any other dog, at a homeless man going through our garbage cans in the alley.'

'Oh, really?' I said in disbelief. 'He really barked? You heard him? For real?'

Neither Gary, nor Cecelia, nor Denise, nor Lauren, nor I had ever heard Chewy bark before: he was a bark-less dog. We all thought it was a little strange but just accepted the fact. I thought it had to do with his breed, or his experience living on the streets. After being in our house for three months, we'd never seen or heard him bark. The dogs next door barked incessantly but Chewy never barked. When Chewy lay in front of my studio and the neighbours' dogs started barking, he got up and moved across the yard into the bushes away from them.

I'd wished he would bark – be a kind of a Lassie guard dog. Turn ferocious and territorial when either Lauren or I were threatened. But Chewy never barked.

Until that Sunday...

'You're not joshing me?' I queried.

'Pleeeease,' Lauren said, contempt in the tone of her voice that even I couldn't miss.

'Really?'

'Yes, he really barked. A small, weak bark like he was trying it out, practising. It seemed as if he was unsure if it was OK to bark. Not knowing quite what to do after barking, he just stood by the fence and looked out through the fence slats at a tall homeless man walking by our garbage cans.'

I noticed Chewy was back by the rear gate, sniffing the gate locks.

'I could hear the lid squeak as the homeless guy lifted the lid of our garbage cans. Maybe Chewy picked up on my displeasure at the man scrounging around in our garbage cans, I don't know. Anyway he barked.'

'Good for him,' I said and looked over at Chewy. 'Good dog, Chewy!' I knew he wouldn't understand what I was saying, but I complimented him anyway. Chewy would know something good had happened by my tone of voice.

It's funny how animals change you.

Lauren looked me in the eye and said, 'I'm thrilled. I'm really glad he barked. Maybe he's thinking of our house as his territory now. Maybe he learned it from the dogs next door. I don't care, I'm excited he barked.'

'Me, too,' I agreed.

And I was. Like Lauren I thought it signalled some kind of transition for Chewy. In the next couple of days, I paid attention, listening for any bark, however weak.

Sure enough, several days later, midweek in the afternoon right after Lauren came home from work, I heard him bark. He was at the rear gate, barking at someone on the other side of our fence. I watched the person's hat bob along the fence top. Our back alleyway is paved. People take short cuts down it: children walking to school, neighbours walking their dogs, homeless routing through garbage for recycling to sell...

Chewy's bark reflected his personality, a medium to high pitch, not particularly scary and not particularly loud.

'It's a bit wimpy,' Lauren chuckled to herself.

We had become so used to Emma's deep-throated defensive growl that made your eyes open wide and feet back up that Chewy's first barks seemed weak in comparison. I squinted my face in concentration. Chewy's body language was right: his head pushed against the fence slats, he rocked back and forth on his paws like he was ready to leap up at the fence. His barks were getting more rapid when I yelled out to him.

'Good dog, Chewy! Good dog! You scared that man away. Good dog, Chewy!'

I tried to infuse my voice with excitement and praise. Lauren joined in. She started clapping in applause. Soon, I was applauding too. Chewy stopped barking. He backed away from the fence and turned his body towards us, looking at us quizzically. His look seem to say, 'Hey, what's up? I'm just doing my job.'

We continued to shout praises and act excited. Chewy's tail went up and started wagging as he wiggle-walked over to us. His rear end seemed detached from his spine as he swung it back and forth. I hoped that was a sign of his happiness.

Again, we both hoped his barking was a sign of his beginning to bond with us, a maturing sign that he thought of our backyard as something to protect, as his home. Neither of us really cared that his barks at first seemed somewhat unsure. They reflected, 'Hey, what's going on out there? I think this is my home but I'm not sure since I've never had a human home. You better leave us alone!' But the barking was Chewy barking, and we were excited to hear his barks.

* * *

Later we were to learn just how ferocious Chewy could be – a surprise to both of us.

One afternoon Lauren and I were walking him along a chainlink fence enclosing a playground yard behind Enslen grammar school. A Pee Wee Baseball game was in progress in the schoolyard. Moms and dads, single parents and family members lined up, cheering their respective teams. Out of nowhere a large grey pit bull was heading straight for us. He leapt at the fence right before us, pushing his snout and face against it. As he seemed friendly, I leaned forward: he was beautiful. Then Chewy came up, pushed against the fence for what looked like a friendly dog greeting separated by the safety of the fence.

The pit bull suddenly started growling low, baring his teeth and aggressively bashing against the fence with his body, tossing and turning his head in what was now rage.

I backed away; Lauren backed away.

But not Chewy!

Suddenly he dived into the fence. Lauren restrained him but in a split second a deep, deep growl came out of his throat and continued along with him baring his teeth and lunging at the other dog.

I was stunned.

Lauren and I gave each other a look that said: 'Wow, where did that come from?' *I don't want to mess with that*, we thought simultaneously. Chewy's bark at times may be weak, his personality gentle and joyous, but push him beyond a certain point and another side of his personality revealed itself: a side that would fight ferociously with a growl as threatening as any I had ever heard.

In that moment, while stunned, both of us gained a new respect for Chewy. His sudden fierceness balanced his personality. In an strange way it also explained another aspect of his behaviour with other dogs. Chewy had an odd kind of confidence around them; few dogs on an individual basis intimidated him. Around larger or more aggressive dogs, while they were sniffing Chewy on first meeting him, all he had to do was to brace his body, set his head in a certain way, throw them a particularly hard glance and emit a low firm growl and the dogs backed off. The growl was nothing like we'd heard at the fence with the pit bull. It was body language, glances and a growl that said: 'I don't play games, now back off!'

To me, these reactions Chewy displayed seem to be a direct result of his experiences on the street as a semi-feral dog. Like a tough street fighter telling someone hassling him: 'If we get into a fight, I'm going to hurt you.'

The remnants of my male chauvinism liked that Chewy had an element of that in him.

* * *

I'm sure Lauren liked it too but for completely different reasons. Because it wasn't long after Chewy started barking along the fence at alley strangers, or up at the front fence when strange people approached our house, that Lauren contacted Donna, our dog trainer.

'Oh, he's changed – he's much more bonded with you,' Donna said in our living room, looking at Lauren. Donna, small and intense, was to the point and direct. I liked her.

'We can work with him now. He's calmer. Your typical mountain-breed types are lovable and easy-going.'

For Lauren and me that was a good sign. It meant Chewy would adapt. Bonding had begun. I was elated, Chewy was bonding with us. Donna had been right to postpone his training – she knew dogs. I looked at Lauren, who was beaming.

Donna would start working with Lauren and Chewy once a week for six weeks. They'd focus on basic good manners, walking on a leash with 'heel', 'sit', 'stay' and 'come' – all standard commands, typical of most basic training.

Getting down to business, Donna had Lauren command, in a strong, clear voice, 'Chewy, come!'

Chewy turned and hid behind the sofa.

'What's going on?' I asked, bewildered.

Before Donna could answer, Lauren said, 'Let me guess. We have seen this before: If you talk too loud, or harsh, Chewy reverts to his street behaviour. He gets scared.'

Suddenly it all made sense: loudness and harshness triggered fear. Then Chewy's street sense took over: escape or avoidance. So, voice commands were tricky: in fact, we spent the entire second training session finding that 'right voice' for Chewy. Lauren had one, I developed another – we both needed to find one that worked for Chewy. And we did. When we found the right voice, Chewy listened.

It was almost as if he was saying, 'I've been waiting a long time for someone to talk to me with respect and love.'

Chapter Twenty
Chewy and Bruce Bond

During the first months of recovery from my two heart attacks I didn't trust my body. Nor did I know my limits. Discovering them was a touchy, difficult and anxiety-producing process.

Walking Chewy was problematic at first. He walked too fast and he was strong; he jerked my arms. Walking him became a day-by-day experiment.

'You ready to go?' Lauren questioned.

I was sitting on the edge of the bed, four months after the heart attacks, taking off my pyjamas and pulling on my blue jeans and T-shirt. Lauren was walking out the front door with Chewy tugging at his leash. She had recovered from her surgery and had returned to work.

'Yeah, yeah, I'll be right there.'

Lauren had given up babying me but I was too prickly even for myself, still angry at my body, frightened and scared that I'd make some stupid mistake that would kill me.

'You can take him,' I said, 'I'm still too weak.'

And I was. Walking out our front door, I locked it and stepped down the front steps. Emerging from under the shade of the sycamore tree, sunlight in my eyes, my mind was contemplating the slight new twinge in my chest: any piercing pain in my pectoral muscle could be a second heart attack. I walked behind Lauren and Chewy over to the canal embankment, dark clouds circling inside my skull. Each successful step was a victory.

To put it mildly, I was depressed. Walking Chewy became a kind of antidote. I watched his butt wiggle, his tail swing and his back leg fluffy pantaloons. He was enjoying himself, every step.

'Are you doing alright?' Lauren would ask, concern in her voice.

Sensitive to the slightest pressure down my arm or tingling in my fingers I would have to judge whether or not I could walk on any particular day. Some afternoons walking was joyous, filled with fresh air, beautiful sunshine and my loving wife. Simply being outside worked wonders. Walking through tree-lined, safe residential neighbourhoods made me realise how blessed I was: I was alive. I could have been dead, I kept telling myself. It was like a vaccination against maudlin self-pity.

Other days it might be too cold, or too windy, or my body simply told me not to walk.

When I began walking Chewy on my own, a few weeks later, his walks became my excuse to exercise myself. What I needed was to rehabilitate my heart emotionally as well as physically

'Chewy, walk?' I'd bark from the back door, scanning the yard for him.

From somewhere in the bushes he'd come veering out into sunlight and then shaking himself off, dust rising above his fur, he'd stand trembling with excitement and his eyes staring up at mine, full of a kind of anticipation, an almost begging look that seemed to say, *Really? Hooray! I've been waiting all day. You did say 'Walk', didn't you? Do you mean it? Really?* Then his body shivered with short, tiny low-keyed whines, one after another.

I'd feel the strange power humans have over dogs, how unfair it was and how dependent he was on me, on us. I was touched.

'Yes, yes,' I'd say. 'Come on, come on!' Then I would retreat into the kitchen to get his leash.

Holding the leash out the back doorway, Chewy would stare at it for a moment and then come bounding into the house, pushing past me, through the kitchen in one swift gallop to get into the front room, where he would turn around and stare back into the dining room to see if I'd followed him. To see if I was really coming and we were going for a walk.

These were strange moments when the responsibility of dog companionship weighed heavily on me. We had basically kidnapped Chewy for our own needs, with good intentions of trying to help him. Now, having another species for which I had accepted responsibility began suddenly to assume proportions I hadn't anticipated. Earlier I had thought of rescuing him mainly to please my wife: where the implications of that rescue would lead, I had no idea.

* * *

'Hold still, hold still,' I said. I was sitting on the living room couch trying to put the leash on him. Chewy was burying his head in between my knees, snorting and throwing his head up playfully. I had grown to enjoy this behaviour, often bending over Chewy's head and talking to him.

'Oh, you're a silly dog, a silly, beautiful doggie!' I would say, my nose near his folded-over ear, whispering foolish endearments into it. If you'd told me twenty years earlier that I'd be whispering 'sweet nothings' into a dog's ear in my mid-sixties, I'd have told you you were nuts. But there I was, and enjoying it. I think Chewy enjoyed it too.

Lauren called it 'humanising' me. Humanising me, bamboozling me, I didn't care.

I started welcoming Chewy inside my studio. He was always attentive and always the gentleman.

'Chewy,' I'd say. 'Come in, Chewy.'

He would look up at the open French doors of my studio, sniff them and with great dignity walk in, coming up to me. He'd put his nose against my outstretched hand and then turn his back to me and lower his body to the cement floor. Drying paints, dirty water, oily pastels and dusty charcoal had become routine smells.

When Chewy first entered the studio, he explored the room, sniffing my supplies. I'd hold out a chunk of compressed vine charcoal, let him sniff it and say, 'Charcoal, Chewy', then I'd turn and point to charcoal drawings pinned to the wall.

'For these,' I'd say, 'I use it for these.' He'd look up as if he understood, glancing at my work (he is a smart dog, after all). Then I'd take a clean piece of paper and demonstrate drawing to Chewy.

In spite of myself, I'd ask his critical opinion: 'Do you like these? Do they remind you of Matisse? Can you see the influence of Cézanne?'

I would like to say that he barked at one drawing and not another; that he led me to a breakthrough. But the truth is, he sniffed my hand, licked it, turned his head away, his glancing eyes averting mine, and simply fell asleep where he was.

Not long after my heart attack, I stopped teaching. During the week, while Lauren is at work, I'm home alone, working six or seven hours in my studio. This lack of human interaction led me to talk to the dogs. Nothing much profound developed except each of us enjoying the other's quiet company. If I had music on and was singing along with the tune, Chewy would stare at me as if trying to comprehend these strange noises humans made. Then, often as not, he'd snort and turn around back towards me and majestically lie down and go to sleep.

'Oh really,' I'd say. 'Your critical acclaim is more delicately expressed than Lauren's. All she says is "boring" and "it's too hot in here, I'm not coming in".'

In late winter Chewy started sleeping most of the day in my studio for the warmth, but the following summer he decided to stay outside because the heat overburdens him, as it does Lauren. After all, he does have thick mountain-dog fur.

For the first few weeks that I allowed Chewy to come into the studio, Fred sat glaring at him and me through the window glass. Fred had been banned from the studio years ago. I'd found he would lie down right on top of my charcoal drawings, thinking this was a great place to sleep. The drawings of course would be damaged. Or he'd decide to sharpen his claws on a wooden frame or paper – normal cat behaviour but devastating to my artwork and expensive art supplies. I couldn't teach him to stop, so he had to stop coming into my studio.

Fred's glare was something neither Chewy nor I would ever forget. Fred hates but accepts these studio limits... to a degree. He does not like being told what to do – after all, he is the King and used to getting what he wants. The minute I become lazy or preoccupied, Fred will sneak into the studio and begin exploring like a stealth bomber. When he is angry with you, he displays his displeasure through body language or some delinquent adolescent action. In cat years Fred is not an adolescent. On the other hand, Chewy is ever the gentleman. As time progressed, when Fred occasionally stared into the studio, Chewy would simply turn his head away, positioning his body between Fred and myself: his body became a visual block. I like to think this is a subtle payback, but I know it isn't true. After all, dogs, if you believe the latest research, aren't capable of that complex an emotion.

Fred sits like a Sphinx, looking into the studio, stunned at my monumental stupidity of allowing a DOG into my studio and not him.

Chapter Twenty-One
A Second Scare

'You're all pasty, pale and white!' Lauren said.

Chewy came jerking me down the sidewalk, excited to return after his walk and see Lauren. It was Saturday afternoon. I faintly smiled. 'Yeah,' I said, 'I don't feel so good – we probably need to go to the hospital.' I handed the leash to Lauren. *Great*, I thought, *just when I'm getting to trust my body again it betrays me.*

Lauren had seen that look before. She was worried – she knew I'd been having small chest pains recently but they went away. The nitro pills helped. But I looked different this time, pasty and white, and I walked very slowly. Lauren agreed about the hospital: something was serious.

The local emergency room doctors wanted to do another angiogram. That would be three in less than nine months, resulting in a lot of scar tissue on my thigh. I insisted the work be done in San Francisco. That way, if the test results indicated further immediate treatment, at least I would be at one of the ten top hospitals in the US.

Strapped on a gurney, the ride to San Francisco hospital was lonely: facing serious health issues focuses your mind. Luckily, Lauren's mother could take care of the animals. At seventy-nine she had been the backup during Lauren's operation and my first heart attack. Now, throughout the three days I was hospitalised in San Francisco, she was the backup once again while Lauren was with me. There had been no time to make other arrangements.

Chewy and Emma would stay at the house, outside during the day and inside at night. Lauren's mom couldn't transport Chewy to the kennel – transporting him back and forth, he might escape. A frightened Chewy was a handful. We felt he had been through too many changes and it was better to leave him where he was comfortable: in our house. He might be lonely for a few days but at least he would be safe. Also, there simply was not enough time for Lauren to make arrangements for him: she had to get to San Francisco.

Rob and Denise would have volunteered to take him but Lauren didn't want to impose on them again. Boss had died unexpectedly a few months earlier and they had a new Rottweiler puppy, Fargo, so their hands were full.

I had the procedure. Everything went well: no new blockage, the stents were clean, the doctor wanted me to stay an extra day to fully recover. For Lauren that meant three full days off work, and two full nights in San Francisco.

* * *

On Tuesday, just as the doctor made his rounds and was talking to me, Lauren got a phone call on her mobile from her mother.

'He what?' Lauren asked, surprised. Everyone turned to look at her.

Embarrassed, she repeated herself in lower tones: 'What happened?' Pointing her finger at the phone, her lips mouthed the words: 'Mom'. She excused herself, and walked across the back of the room and down the hall.

Lying in bed, my eyes followed her as she left. The doctor explained that in cases like mine, the cause of my chest pains was unknown but most likely just severe transitory angina. Staying an extra day meant a fuller recovery.

'Not to worry,' the doctor said. 'You're on blood thinners and a drip. We contacted your cardiologist here at UCSF and got all your records. All the tests were negative so right now all we can do is keep an eye on your vital signs and wait for tomorrow morning to discharge you safe and sound.'

He smiled and gave me a little pat on my hand. The pat probably reassured the doctor that they were doing everything possible. *It's out of my hands now*, I thought, watching the white coat of the doctor walk away. *This great teaching hospital gives me some of the best doctors available in Northern California, that's all I can do right now*. I knew my medications were helping to reduce the anxiety, but I wondered what was going on, not only with my heart but also with Lauren and her phone call.

A few moments after the doctor left, Lauren came back in the room. 'Mom called. Chewy has escaped again,' she said, obviously worried.

'Mom was upset,' Lauren went on as she sat down. 'I tried to calm her down but she knows how much Chewy means to us.'

Chewy had escaped out the front door again – he's a smart one. Denise rang the front door buzzer while Lauren's mother was at our house taking care of the animals. She explained that she had stopped by to see how Chewy was doing and to offer help, if needed.

Denise and Lauren's mother, Barbara, were talking with the screen door between them. The screen door wasn't latched.

As Lauren talked, I imagined Chewy stretching as he got up, eyes on the door, his hind legs and paws stiffening as the stretch moved through his body. *Who is this?* he probably thought. *I recognise that smell.* He slowly walked over to the door, coming up unseen behind Barbara. Then seeing the open door and screen, the opportunity for escape must have lit up his frontal lobes like a billboard.

Escape! His eyes widened and with the silence of a stealth bomber Chewy sidestepped Lauren's mother, nudged the black screen door open just enough and so quickly that before Denise and Barbara noticed its sudden movement he had already pushed past them, scampering down the front steps onto the sidewalk and freedom.

Ha! he probably thought when he looked back at the two stunned women – Denise turning around, Lauren's mother stepping out onto the porch. The mouths of both of them opening into a yell: 'Chewy! Chewy!'

He'd heard that frantic high-pitched tone before. All it meant was trouble. Chewy stopped on the sidewalk in front of the house for a second and a second glance at the waving and shouting women, and then he was gone.

Lauren knew her mother was overwhelmed with guilt. Barbara knew how much Chewy meant to her daughter: she knew how much time and energy had gone into rescuing him. She also knew how upset Lauren had been when Chewy had escaped the first time but she never thought Chewy could be THAT sneaky. She had underestimated him.

Lauren tried to calm her mother, telling her it would be OK. *OK*, Lauren thought to herself, *how do I know that? OK, if he doesn't get hit by a car? Or get killed? Or be gone forever?* As she tried to calm her mother down, Lauren thought Chewy would eventually need to decide what he wanted to do: stay in our house or possibly someplace else, if only the street. Lauren told her mother that she could not come back to Modesto to look for Chewy, that it was more important that she should stay in San Francisco with me and be available to talk to the various doctors.

She suggested that her mother call Cecelia to see if she could help. Cecelia would want to know that Chewy had escaped again, anyway. Cecelia, if she could, would go looking for him.

When Barbara called, she left a message with Cecelia's sister, Charlotte, as Cecelia was still working. But Denise helped immediately; Denise hoped she might see Chewy and bring him home, as she and Lauren had done the last time he escaped. She hurried home, got into her car and drove around the neighbourhood looking and calling out for Chewy. She drove around Gracaeda Park and past the canal bridge on West Morris Avenue and then by Gary's house. After an hour with no sign of Chewy she drove home.

Meanwhile, Barbara locked the back and front doors and began walking up Magnolia Avenue, looking for Chewy. 'Chewy, Chewy,' she cried out. *Oh, this won't do*, she thought to herself. *No luck at all, this is hopeless*!

Since it was almost lunchtime, Barbara drove back to her own house, made herself some lunch and rested. Thinking about everything, she decided the best thing to do was to go back to Bruce and Lauren's house. She would simply sit on the front porch in the swing with a mystery book to read and wait. If anything happened, she would be there. She resolved to stay and read, hoping Chewy would come back. The front door was open; only the screen door was shut. She wouldn't make a mistake this time.

The swing was comfortable; pillows propped up her back, the porch and the sycamore trees provided shade.

An hour went by. Then around three o'clock, third and fourth graders walked by with backpacks bigger than they were dangling off their shoulders. Neighbours walking their dogs waved.

Late in the afternoon while Barbara was reading, Chewy came strolling down the sidewalk behind some children. Barbara couldn't believe her eyes; she wanted to shout his name out but decided that might scare him. As if he owned the neighbourhood, as if he had just been on a quiet little stroll (which from his perspective perhaps he had been), as if nothing had happened, he turned up the driveway, came up the front steps, a grace in his step, and then looked over at Lauren's mother as a signal for her to get up and open the screen door. He sat down before the screen door while Barbara, scrambling to put her mystery novel down and recovering her composure, got up quietly and walked over to the screen door and opened it.

When she opened the screen door, Chewy looked up at her as if to say thank you but he didn't bark, didn't wag his tail or lick her hand. He simply stood up, tail high, and walked in as if he owned the place – and from a certain perspective he most surely did.

It had been an exciting jaunt but Chewy was tired and hungry. He walked into the back bedroom where his dog bed was, stopped for water and crashed. He'd been gone four or five hours. Who knew where he'd gone or what he'd done? Dogs have their secrets – secrets it's better humans don't know about.

Barbara called Lauren to let her know Chewy was safe and sound in the house. He would be waiting for them when they got home the next day. Unfortunately, she forgot to call Cecelia to let her know Chewy was safe at home. Cecelia had no way of contacting Lauren's mother. When she got home from work, her sister told her what had happened. Cecelia changed clothes and walked the four blocks over to our house in the hope that Barbara would be there. Cecelia was worried: this was Chewy's third escape. Oh, he was such a good boy but such a bad doggie! *What's with that dog?* she wondered. *Lauren and Bruce are wonderful parents, they love Chewy so much.*

When she got to the house, she could see no one was home. She didn't know whether Chewy was inside. Cecelia rang the front door bell; it woke Chewy up. He came to the front door but Cecelia couldn't see him because the blinds were down. But Chewy could smell Cecelia; he sniffed around the curtains and door.

The front room curtains were down, but at the bottom left-side window there was a small space where a knot in the curtain cord stopped the curtain from fully dropping. Cecelia noticed this. She got down on her hands and knees, peering through this small sliver of window to see if Chewy was in the house. Chewy meanwhile wondered what the heck was going on: when he looked down, he saw Cecelia's round, brown soft eye staring through the sliver of window. He knew the smell, but he didn't know what that rolling thing was.

Cecelia rolled her eye in its orb, trying to make out what was before her; she saw red fur – maybe it was Chewy, maybe Emma (Emma had red fur too). She pushed her eye and cheek closer to the window but couldn't make out any distinct form. As Cecelia was crawling around on our front porch trying to determine if Chewy was indeed in the house, she heard a voice behind her.

Cecelia froze. She didn't get up immediately because she needed a moment. *This was awkward*, she thought to herself. *What am I going to say?*

'Do you need help?' the voice asked.

The voice sounded gentle enough but you never knew. Cecelia pushed herself back up on the heels of her walking shoes. Steadying herself with her left hand, she rose up before the glass window, adjusting her waist jacket and turned.

Ben, who lived next door, had a warm, open face. He stood a foot and a half taller than Cecelia and when she looked up into his face, he was smiling.

'A little odd, don't you think?' he said. 'Crawling around on someone's front porch.'

Oh God, Cecelia thought, *this is going to be really awkward*. Before she could say anything, Ben said. 'Janie, my wife and I noticed you. We figured you must know Lauren. Janie sent me over to see if you needed any help.'

Well, Cecelia thought, *that's a relief. What nice neighbours, I'm in luck.*

She explained what she was doing and why to Ben. 'Let me help,' he said, dropping to his knees. Pushing his blond hair off his forehead, he flattened his cheek and eye socket against the window, peering in.

Chewy jumped back. He heard all the voices outside the front door; he heard the doorknob turn when Ben's hand grabbed it to check that it wasn't open. It was dark inside the front room and Chewy wondered what the heck was going on. He threw his paws forward and stared at the sliver of light. Now he was two feet from the door; he didn't bark. Emma didn't even come into the front room. The cats, attracted by the commotion, were parading one by one into the front room, their curiosity aroused.

'I can't see anything,' Ben said.

'Don't you see red fur?' Cecelia responded.

'Red fur?'

'Yes, red fur! Chewy has red fur.' Cecelia, impatient with men, pushed Ben aside. 'Let me look again.'

She bent down, squished her eye against the glass and peered in. 'Yes, red fur. It's as plain as the nose on your face. Can't you see it?'

Ben threw his eye against the window. *Well, yes, there was something there. It could be red fur but I don't know*, he thought to himself. *Maybe she's right*.

Fred then walked by the window.

'I see something moving,' Ben said.

Chewy stood up. *Humans*, he thought.

A Second Scare

After a bit, Cecelia and Ben both agreed a red furry dog was inside the house and most likely it was Chewy. Cecelia felt certain that Chewy was safe. She shook Ben's hand, thanked him and walked back home.

They were right: Chewy was inside the house. He had escaped and come back. This time he'd been gone for four hours, not the entire day as he had been in April.

Chapter Twenty-Two
Not Again!

A week later, Lauren was still thinking about Chewy's latest adventure. She was fed up with his escapades.

Her dream of a dog at her feet wasn't happening.

Chewy's escapes just didn't make sense for he seemed to want to come back. Lauren knew he was still adjusting to his new life but at the same time he wasn't a Siberian husky with the genetic instinct to roam. She knew the back-yard was small, but Chewy got an hour's walk almost daily, sometimes twice-daily and on weekends, she took him for two-hour walks. He seemed to have adjusted to Fred and the cats, Emma was no problem so why run away?

But Chewy had started to bond. Both Lauren and I could pet him without him being upset; his stress panting had stopped. He followed some commands and was learning others; he was eating regularly. Now he even came in regularly at night without issue – most of the time. Bonding was definitely taking place.

Lauren looked at Chewy, who was sitting on the kitchen floor (Sunday mornings in our house were always slow).

'You've started to accept us, haven't you, Chewy?'

Chewy was waiting for his food, sitting among the cats while Lauren was feeding them. Fred was licking his fur nonchalantly. Chewy sat on the other side of the kitchen floor. There were three large tubs of cat food between them.

'Where's the paper?' I asked. I was sitting at the breakfast nook table, cereal and soya milk before me. I was reading the nutritional label on the dry cereal. Since my heart attacks I'd checked everything for cholesterol and sodium levels.

He's a little obsessive, Lauren thought, *but he's my obsessive.*

'Do you want me to get it?' I asked, looking over at her.

She had an empty cat bowl in her hand. 'No, I'm up. I'll get it.'

I looked at her. She was in her pyjamas, her grey hair squished up into a Mohawk. *She's sweet. A little obsessive, but she's my obsessive.*

Lauren put the empty cat food bowl down, waded through the five cats past the dining room table and into the front room. Chewy followed. I watched his tail held high disappear out the kitchen door.

This cereal is really good, I thought to myself. No cholesterol, low sodium and thirteen grams of protein – that's as much protein as an egg. I poured little squares and crinkly rice, soya grits and red wheat into the white cereal bowl. Then, after pouring the milk, I heard the shout.

'No, not again, Chewy! Not again!' Lauren's voice easily carried to the kitchen. 'You know, I'm getting real tired of this,' she exclaimed.

I heard the front door screen slam. Then it opened again.

'Come on, Chewy. Come on! Come inside, pleeeeease,' Lauren's voice was pleading. 'Let's have a nice Sunday morning, Chewy.'

On the sidewalk before the front door where he had stopped and turned the sunlight fell across Chewy's head and shoulders. His tail was a red flag waving in the wind. Perplexed and angry, Lauren stood in the front door frame, pleading with him.

Chewy just looked at her, turned and started walking down the sidewalk, ready for another adventure.

'OK, CHEWY, THAT'S IT! I'M TIRED OF THIS! I want to have a nice Sunday morning. I'm not coming after you this time. Chewy, you need to decide if this is going to be your home or not – YOU decide!'

Chewy took off down the street.

Lauren latched the screen door and as it was a beautiful warm October morning, she left the front door open. She turned around, walking back into the house. When she came into the kitchen and before I could ask, she said, 'You'll never guess what just happened?'

She sat down across from me. I knew this tone: a mixture of bitter disappointment, being morally wronged and hurt permeated her voice. I had a spoonful of 'Save My Heart' cereal in my mouth and choked on it.

'That dog,' Lauren said, 'he took off again. Escaped. This time it was my fault.'

She explained that she thought she could just open the doors and reach out in her pyjamas and grab the Sunday newspaper, which had been thrown close to the front door. As she did so Chewy was right beside her. Lauren, anxious to see what the headline said, had snatched off the rubber band around the paper and unfolded it with both hands. Her eyes read the headlines and she was distracted for thirty seconds. Chewy saw his opportunity and went for it; he pushed his shoulders past Lauren's thigh before she felt him and was down the front steps before she realised what had happened.

'I wanted to go after him but when I started, I realised I'd had it with his escapes: I want a nice, quiet Sunday morning, not a big drama. I got mad and told him he'd better make up his mind: either he chooses to be with us or not, it's his decision. I'm frustrated and hurt.'

I was slightly stunned. As we were talking in the kitchen, Lauren heard a little whimpering.

'Did you hear that?' She thought it sounded like a dog, but couldn't be certain.

'Hear what?' I asked.

'That?' There it was again. She got up and walked into the front room.

She saw a little miracle at the front door: Chewy was behind the screen, whining to get back into the house.

Lauren was astonished – it had been ten minutes since he'd escaped.

She was elated.

'Oh, you're such a good boy, Chewy!' she said, pushing the screen door open. Then Chewy bounded in, into her open arms. She kissed and hugged him, rubbing her fingers through his mane and along his body. Chewy wiggled his hindquarters and snaked his body into an 'S'. He looked up at Lauren, trying to lick her face.

'Oh, my good, good doggie, Chewy boy!' Lauren murmured to him.

She was ecstatic.

In the kitchen, I could imagine from the commotion what had happened. When Lauren's left foot came through the hallway door, Chewy pushed past. I got up, the cats scattered; Lauren pushed the cat food containers back and we started jumping up and down, waving our arms, shouting 'Hurray!' and 'Good dog, Chewy!' Sensing the excitement, Chewy looked up, his head and eyes first on Lauren and then on me, and then as Lauren chanted his name, back on her. The celebration lasted a good ten minutes till I begged off, saying, 'Laurie, my heart can't take it!' I sat down at the kitchen table a bit winded, but laughing and smiling all the same.

Lauren gave Chewy an extra-special food treat: all the wet food he wanted and his favourite chicken jerky. When she sat down, Chewy lay at her feet as she began to read the newspaper. She had her nice quiet Sunday morning after all: her husband across from her, reading how the San Francisco 49ers were doing and her dog at her feet, chewing on chicken jerky. She pushed her spoon into her yogurt, drank her freshly brewed coffee and scanned the paper for half-off sales on women's shoes.

With a spoonful of creamy smooth yogurt on her tongue and looking out the breakfast room window, she was sure Chewy had made his decision. Our house was his home. Finally!

All day long Lauren gave Chewy extra love and attention. She was convinced Chewy's return was the final turning point in his acceptance of his new life.

If only it were that easy.

Chapter Twenty-Three
Bruce's Experiment

Chewy lay with his white muzzle over the edge of the cellar door, his body collapsed in boredom behind him. I pushed my studio door open. His brown eyes rolled left, following me.

Most weekdays, at 4 p.m., I exercised: first, a walk and then a series of light weights. Chewy knew the routine. When the lock clicked on my studio door, his folded ears straightened. Head raised, his mouth opened into what I took to be a smile of anticipation.

'No, Chewy,' I said, 'not now.'

Chewy's head collapsed back on his paws. His eyes rolled away and then turned back, looking directly at me.

They seemed to say: 'For God's sake take me for a walk – I'm bored out of my mind!'

This look always moved me deeply. Call it guilt, call it anthromorphising or empathy, call it simple caring for someone you're responsible for, all I really know is that then and there I decided I had to improve his quality of life. But I had no clear idea how.

The first thing that happened was this: right then I took him for a walk. Excited, he almost yanked my arm out of its socket. He wanted to sniff on one side of the street and then the other; up people's driveways and down in the bushes along their front porches. At some houses, if I let him he would have dragged me into the backyard.

I got into several tug of wars when he wanted to go one way and I wanted to go the other. As I yanked and pulled on his leash I realised this wasn't any fun. I began to have a bunch of small realisations that led to a much bigger change.

Excitement was gone from Chewy's life. Leaning his full bodyweight at the end of the leash in a direction I didn't want to go, he gave me glances that seemed to say: 'What's wrong with you? What's the big deal? Let's go this way!' Sometimes we couldn't: for example, crossing the middle of the street into oncoming traffic. Other times, like sniffing down the side of someone's house, social customs prohibited. But then it dawned on me: we went on the same boring walk every time we walked together; down the same street, turn at the same corner, at about the same time of day. It was a routine that fitted only my needs.

I didn't have a clue what Chewy's needs might be. In some unclear sense I realised our rescuing Chewy had also enslaved him. Of course, the alternative to his being rescued would most likely have been his death. Animal control catching him could have put him up as an adoptable pet but the odds were against his adoption: his skittishness, shyness and withdrawal would have worked against him. Most likely he would have been euthanised or if adopted, returned. Or perhaps let loose back again into the streets.

Our motives, Lauren's and mine, were relatively altruistic: we simply wanted to help him. But the reality is that to rescue him, we drugged him. And once we'd rescued him, we used force again: whether a fence, a leash or providing and then withholding food. In Chewy's case we also neutered him: for our needs, not his.

And then after doing all that, we wanted him to 'bond' with us; to 'love' us. To be a certain kind of 'dog', to come in at night for eight to ten hours, to be in our backyard with cats and another dog. Also, at best to get one hour every day to walk at the end of a leash wherever we wanted for our exercise. Had he been another human being, our behaviour would have been outrageous, criminal even.

He was another species: a species that had emotions – felt pain, got excited, looked at times to be happy – a species with a certain degree of cognitive capacity. With Chewy, I was locked into a set of relationships that I had never thought about. Lauren was much more certain about the fairness and justice of her relations with him. All I really knew was that I wanted to maximise his free-thinking abilities and his sphere of freedom within our relationship of living in a medium-sized American city with my wife.

What that meant I really didn't know: how to treat Chewy I would have to discover.

* * *

After reading around the subject, I started to change my behaviour in two ways. First, I began 'explaining things' to Chewy, an idea I got from Ted Kerasote, in his book *Merle's Door*. I'd hold an object up to Chewy, name it, repeat the name and then allow him to sniff it.

Earlier, when I was explaining objects in the studio, my desire was to bond with Chewy. Now those explanations were meant to enhance his daily experience, to create some excitement, some curiosity and spark his interest.

Sometimes Lauren thought I was nuts.

For example, when Chewy came up, sniffing our table food, I held out a piece of tofu before his nostrils and said, 'Tofu, Chewy – it's what I eat for protein.'

If he tried to lick the tofu, I said, 'No, Chewy. It's only for me – it's human food.'

His eyes looked up at me and then he turned his head away.

Lauren's eyes looked at me, her mouth opened as if she was going to say something and then her lips closed around a tight-lipped smile. Her frown said: *You poor, crazy man, you're nuts but you're very sweet.*

I have no illusion that Chewy understood anything of what I said, but with his food and toys, I did the same thing. In my studio, when he came in, I let him sniff my paintbrushes and I explained what they were. Then, as he settled down, I let him watch me paint in my studio. At times he watched, other times he simply turned away or walked back out of the studio.

Let me tell you sometimes I felt pretty foolish explaining the use of a paint brush to a dog and then demonstrating its use to him. And I don't have any clue that it increased his intelligence – I'm sure it didn't except in the sense that it gave him new smells and new experiences for whatever that was worth to the development of canine intelligence.

Brushes didn't always interest him but food always did: salmon burgers in particular. Alizarin crimson, a beautiful colour I used, bombed with Chewy: his sniff lasted less than three seconds. Carrots, he spat out. Art books, even with full-colour illustrations, held no interest for him: he simply sniffed and turned away. 'Nude Descending a Staircase', the famous icon in the art world, left him cold. (On that we both agreed.)

But I was, and am, willing to try on the off-chance, the outlying chance, that changes might occur; that such experiences might spark neural changes. When I imagined myself and the angels in heaven sitting on clouds at the right hand of God and all of us looking down at me in my studio, explaining to Chewy about brushes, colours and the 'Nude Descending a Staircase', I knew we were all shaking our heads and laughing uproariously, but I didn't mind. So long as I didn't have to go and defend myself on *Meet the Press* or *Charlie Rose*, or before David Letterman. This was just between Chewy and me, *mano en mano*.

After two months, I began to explain fewer new things to him. Predominately food and cloths still interested him. I find it fascinating now that when I'm doing something new, Chewy comes up to sniff and see what I'm doing, almost as if he's entitled to do so – he just wants to check things out. Sometimes he actually comes up and nudges my hand or elbow when I'm doing something, almost as if to say: 'Hey, what's going on?' or 'Let me see, boss'.

The second and bigger change was 'sniff walks'. I hated the idea of a dog on a leash, but I understand and accept the necessity of leashes in cities. It's the law, and cars could kill Chewy. The more time he spent with us, the more he seemed to lose much of his car street sense. Often he'd try to pull Lauren or me into the street on his walks, even if a car was coming.

But Chewy on a leash still rankled me. How would I like being leashed? Dog behaviourist Dr Patricia McConnell, in her book *The Other End of the Leash*, advocates sniff walks. She inspired me to try them with Chewy.

Lauren, following our trainer's advice, initially kept Chewy on a short leash, at her side, walking slightly behind her. She called it the 'heel walk'. But Chewy never performed well under that routine, so she gave him much more leash but still controlled the pace, the leash length, the time and basically, the direction of his walks.

I explained 'sniff walks' to her and discussed my intent to experiment with them. 'Fine,' she said tensely.

I felt foolish explaining to Chewy what I was about to do with this wild experiment. He simply looked up at me for a moment and then turned away. I knew my changed behaviour would be the critical factor.

On the day of the first sniff walk, everything went according to our routine until we stopped at the end of the driveway: here was where Chewy got to take control. He sat down in the centre of the driveway waiting for me to indicate which direction to go. I was at his side, slightly behind him. The afternoon sun shone on both of us; the sky was blue and clear of clouds. I looked up, avoiding eye contact with him.

'Which way, Chewy?' I asked. I would like to tell you that he jumped up, barked in glee and took off decidedly to the right or left but the reality was he just looked confused. He sat looking forwards for a short period of time, then looked up at me and finally turned left and walked back behind me on my right side. Then he sat down slightly behind me on the cement driveway.

I took this behaviour to indicate that he knew the old rules – Bruce leads, Chewy follows. But this time Bruce didn't lead; Bruce just stood there. Chewy seemed confused. Undoubtedly he was. He stood up, did a tight little circle at my feet, looked up at me and then sat back down again – waiting, I suppose, for my body language to suggest a direction.

My right leg started to move. *Don't*, I told myself. Uneasy, anxiety swept over me; I had to fight the urge to take control. I looked away, staring up into the tree branches. Then I heard Chewy below me, squirming. When I turned to make eye contact with him, I stopped myself and took a deep breath. Exhaling relaxed me. I stood quietly, suppressing any body language clues about which direction to go – right or left, or back into the house.

Minutes went by. Anxious and impatient my mind flooded with excuses to take back control. My body fidgeted. My legs twitched. I tensed my body, and fought the temptation to look down at Chewy. What was he thinking? What was I thinking? Why was this so hard?

Objectively I was probably fidgeting. Chewy certainly was when I glanced down sideways at him. Several times I said: 'Which way, Chewy?' or 'Your choice, Chewy'. As if he could understand. The unfairness of the whole situation was getting to me.

I have no illusions he understood those words, or that instruction. After what seemed a very long time, when I found myself wondering what the neighbours seeing me standing in the middle of my driveway with a dog circling my calves might think. A man standing in his driveway with his dog for fifteen minutes asking the dog which way did he want to go? It must have seemed strange.

Luckily no one came out to ask what I was doing, and no strangers walked by our house to stare at Chewy and me. No curious stray dogs came by to sniff.

Then, magically, Chewy stood up and took off to the left. The leash snapped taut, his rhythm quickened. My arms jerked left and we were off. I started a little pitter-patter run, like a little old person's shuffle, because Chewy's pace was quicker than mine. My heart rate couldn't exceed 90 bpm and I hadn't run in five years. I wondered how long I could keep up with his pace.

Off we went under the sycamore trees – a dog pulling his master at the other end of a leash. I loved the irony. I thought of McConnell's book title: *The Other End of the Leash* as Chewy jerked me along: now I was at the other end of the leash with Chewy leading the way.

Chewy sniffed the first tree he came to – a long head sniff at the base of the tree, then on to the next one. I felt like a top being spun around at the end of a string. Not that I minded, I simply wasn't used to either the pace or the length of Chewy's sniffs. It required patience to stop every few feet in order to let him sniff and explore where he wanted to.

We went tree to tree, bush to plant, tree to stub grass, to squashed poo, crumpled paper in the street, back to a tree trunk and the base of a big bush where Chewy peed and sprayed. And finally stopped. He simply stood head high up in the air and sniffed.

Chewy's exuberance was exhilarating. I was being

pulled along but I was happy and curious, thinking he was excited. Perhaps tasting freedom, relatively speaking, for the first time in ages. I wondered where all this would lead. Did he have secret paths, houses he loved, people and dogs he knew that I might get introduced to?

Up sidewalks, down along houses, onto front porches, into bushes; stopping at garbage containers, peering into fences... Now a sudden spin around for a second, deeper sniff; jags across streets, squats under bushes... Then suddenly he jags across a street or squats under a bush again. For the first twenty minutes the exhilaration overwhelmed my sense of propriety and any concerns about how fast my pulse was climbing.

I knew in the first few minutes that sniff walks wouldn't be anything like our ordinary walks, particularly if I gave Chewy as much freedom as I possibly could, short of letting him off the leash. The random helter-skelter nature of the walk made me realise that on his own Chewy explored the streets differently from our sedentary walks. He must have been glad of those forty-five-minute walks but in reality they were nothing like his own free saunters down our city streets. I also knew he deserved to be off-leash frequently, if only in a limited-size doggie park.

After the first twenty minutes of this relatively free roaming my heart was begging for mercy; I had to stop. Chewy was unhappy with this.

'I'm sorry, Chewy,' I told him, not out of breath but worried about my heart. 'I'm too old – I have to stop and rest.'

We parked ourselves under a tree at a cross walk. Chewy gazed at me, panting and smiling for the longest time. At least it seemed like the longest time. The reality was I closed my eyes, looking at him and rested my head against the tree trunk. When I opened them, Chewy's head was surveying the street, turning left and right. Lying on his stomach completely relaxed, yet very alert. His semi-feral behaviour or ancestors' genetics were fully engaged.

Chewy was ready to follow his nose again and so we took off for a second instalment. He took me down alleys we had never gone into, up streets we'd never visited, he sniffed fences, we stuck our heads through them, carefully reconnoitred fences with barking and growling pit bulls behind them, stepped in puddles, dog poo, cooled our feet in flowing water along kerbs and followed the irrigation canal further than we'd ever done when I controlled the walks.

Given the chance, Chewy had no problem taking control: he varied the pace, direction, time, duration and ultimately the meaning of the walks, or at least the meaning of part of the walks.

The first sniff walks were a terrific success. Chewy had taken the lead – he controlled the walk to a much greater extent than his normal walks. So, did he enjoy it? Well, I'm biased. I think he did. Can I prove it? No.

Repeated walks revealed even more unexpected results: Chewy developed routines. His first routines appeared to reveal patterns of behaviour from before he was rescued. He repeatedly walked back to what Lauren and I took to be the boundaries of his old territory. Not that our sense of his stray environment was necessarily accurate.

When he walked along the canal path, he seemed to want to walk further down than we thought his territory extended. The same was true on the west side of his territory. On the south side, he wanted to cross a very busy street that led him back downtown and across a major highway into a territory where dogs roamed unleashed and in larger packs.

It might have been nothing more than simple exploratory behaviour and a high degree of curiosity. I thought it might be about visiting old haunts. He went back again and again to a particularly vicious and barking pit bull locked behind a chain-linked fence. Each visit, the pit bull came charging and barking at the fence but each time Chewy merely sniffed the fence before his barking face. The pit bull followed Chewy down the fence, barking and snarling until Chewy walked beyond the fence. The other dog was left snapping mad and growling into the corner of the fence. But Chewy never looked back – he just kept walking.

As mentioned earlier, Chewy had had an aggressive encounter with another pit bull in the school-yard at

Enslen School. Why he chose to be aggressive with that particular dog but to walk away from the pit bull in the backyard of a neighbour's house I never understood.

'May I help you?' was a common question from home-owners who came out to greet me as Chewy wandered up their sidewalk towards their front porch. None of them knew Chewy but I had the distinct impression he knew their houses, or perhaps their dogs. Some of the houses had cat food on the front porch or littered in small piles around the front yard. During tough times Chewy may have poached their cat food or water, or even both.

The wildness of the walks quickly led to limits I felt I had to impose: no wild cutting across busy streets, no walking up sidewalks to people's front porches, no walking down the sides of people's houses and no entering backyards by holes in alley fences. I didn't mind the zig-zag nature of his walks but peeing on a home-owners' prize rose bushes simply wasn't acceptable, nor was spreading his scent by digging up grass with his paw scratches. Most of the time I had no idea why he did what he did on those sniff walks except perhaps he was following his nose, his curiosity and sense of adventure.

Following him was my adventure. One day a large elderly golden retriever lay sprawled on his stomach on the grass in the front yard of his home. Chewy stopped dead in his tracks and looked up at me.

We stood in silence for a moment, trying to figure out what was going on with the other dog. Chewy didn't move; the retriever didn't move. His hair was all matted up, his body looked collapsed; his breathing was slow and irregular. After several minutes of silence, the dog's owner, a heavy-set, middle-aged man, came out and explained he had just set his elderly dog outside on the grass – the dog loved to lie in the sun. He was dying, the owner said, and they were actually on their way to the vets; his long-time companion was about to be euthanised. The man was close to tears as he spoke and excused himself to go back into the house.

All this time Chewy sat extremely still. He didn't pull on the leash or bark, but sat quietly as if honouring the scene or at least recognising the gravity of the situation. I know that is probably projecting but I felt sad and thought of how elephants mourn their dead in silent homage. After a while, the man came back out to the front yard to attend to his dog. In deference to him and his companion, I gave Chewy's leash a gentle pull and we walked on.

The sniff walks proved to be a great experiment. Initially they exhausted me. Slowly, as I grew fitter, they became fun. Guilt and obligation to Chewy motivated me to walk when my will failed; he kept me going, I was healing. Walking the neighbourhood was always an adventure with Chewy leading.

Over time I discovered the boundary between giving Chewy his freedom and the real limits of living in a city. On these walks he seems much happier. One fun discovery was to learn how much of a creature of habit

Chewy actually is. He showed me several routines he used to negotiate the city and together we explored the boundaries of his feral territory.

They may not be walks every dog owner is comfortable with but for Lauren and me, they work. At home I now look forward to them.

Chewy does, too.

Chapter Twenty-Four
Again, Really?

I heard the knock on the door. I knew something was up because the gardener rarely knocks a second time after I've let him in the front gate. His dark shadow outside the front door swayed, rocking on his heels.

I opened the door.

The gardener stepped back and spoke quickly before I could say anything.

'HE WHAT?'

'He got out the front gate,' our gardener said. He looked sheepish, having been outfoxed by a dog. 'He's a smart one! He was waiting by the front gate; the minute I opened the gate to push my lawnmower through, he was out. He scooted right behind my back when I turned to close the gate. I barely saw him before he was gone.'

I looked at him incredulously. We stood just inside the front door frame; shadows darkened his face. *Oh no, not again*! I thought. Chewy hadn't escaped for so long – I thought we were over this.

'Which way did he go?' I asked the gardener.

'Down to the left, and I briefly followed him but he turned down the alley and I lost him. He's a lot faster than he looks.'

I panicked. *Better call Lauren*, I thought. *Better go try to find him first, though. How far can he go?* I wondered.

'He's been gone about ten minutes,' the gardener said.

I walked down the alley. The black and green garbage bins were empty and knocked over in the alley; garbage had been collected two hours earlier. Now the smells were gone. Sunflowers grew along and against our fence. Squashed grapefruit pulverised by the giant tyres of the garbage truck lay smeared across the alley asphalt. Rob and Denise's new dog, Fargo, barked at me as I walked by, shouting: 'Chewy, Chewy!'

When I stepped out onto the sidewalk at the end of the alley, Chewy was nowhere to be seen. Our gardener had left and walked two houses down to his house. I could hear him working in his backyard.

Crap, I thought, *now what am I going to tell Lauren?* I walked back down the alley and went home, upset.

When I called Lauren at work she said: 'HE WHAT?' Then her voice dropped. 'I thought we were over that.'

I could hear someone coming into her office at the other end of the phone. 'Oh look,' she said, 'someone just came in – I've got to go. Just leave it alone. He's got to figure this out for himself: whether he wants to go or stay. I thought he had decided but maybe he needs a reminder. Who knows?'

This was a little too cavalier for me but who knew? Besides Chewy was her dog.

Anxiety stalked me like the plague for the next hour and a half. I tried painting but my mind always wandered back to what was happening with Chewy. Though I tried telling myself that Lauren knew best, I still worried. I tried making up some health drinks in the blender but that was only a stop-gap measure. Finally, after reading also failed, I slipped into a jacket and went outside, intent on walking over to the canal to see if Chewy was there, and if not, walking down to Graceada Park, checking for him there. I told myself the search could also double for my afternoon walk for my heart and if I found him, so much the better. I wanted him home so Lauren wouldn't have to deal with finding him again.

When I locked the front door and stepped down the front steps I remembered that I had forgotten the leash and collar. How would I bring him home without that?

After retrieving them, I started walking down our street, Magnolia Avenue, towards the canal. Bright sunlight broke through the trees. When I looked up the street, I couldn't believe my eyes: Chewy was sitting at the end of the block across the busy traffic on West Morris Avenue at the corner, looking directly at me.

Elated, I shouted, 'Chewy!'

He looked up just as two cars sped by in front of him. *Oh no*, I thought, *if he runs out into the street he'll get himself killed*.

I know this sounds crazy but I started to hide. I stepped sideways off the concrete sidewalk behind the grey tan bark of the big sycamore trunk in front of our house. With my back against the tree, my thinning hair caught in the edges of the bark. *Great*, I thought, *I can't afford to lose any more of my hair – I'm almost bald as it is. I can't run down the block, shouting his name because he'd most likely step into traffic and get himself killed. Besides, I can't run fast enough to get to the corner before he might move.*

I stuck my balding head out from around the edge of the tree, neck curled around the bark like a snake, trying to see Chewy. He was still there. Still sitting quietly, looking every which way, seemly unaware of me. I felt like Peter Sellers creeping up on the bad guys in the Pink Panther movies. Only Chewy wasn't a bad guy, I wasn't Peter Sellers, and this wasn't a movie.

Then I spied the nearest car, an old Buick, parked on the street. I could creep over to it when Chewy turned his head and get there before he saw me. I was worried that seeing me would cause him to lunge out into the busy traffic only to get whacked by a car or truck. So I tiptoed over to the trunk of the maroon-coloured Buick and hunched down, sweating. All the while I prayed none of the neighbours had seen me. I didn't want to have to explain myself – even if I could concoct a reasonable explanation.

Chewy was still there; the traffic was still speeding by. Why did the traffic have to be so busy today on West

Morris? When Chewy looked away again, I dashed as best I could to the right and across our neighbours' grass to the parked white Honda in the driveway, two houses from our front door. Luckily, the neighbours in whose yard and driveway I was trespassing were not home, otherwise they might come out the door and start yelling at me. The yelling would certainly upset Chewy as he was close enough to hear and see.

Now, I only had the duplex unit located at the end of the street to negotiate. Chewy was still sitting on the corner. Amazed he hadn't moved or noticed me sneaking around, I wondered what the hell was going through his mind. I never considered the possibility that he had already smelled me and knew I was coming. He might wonder what this crazy human was doing, sneaking from a tree trunk to a car and then to another car. Finally, with my back flat along the side of the duplex unit, I was sliding closer to him.

Did he really think I didn't see him crouched and hiding behind the big bush at the corner of the rental unit? Chewy might wonder. *Silly humans!*

So I leaned my back against the plastered wall of the duplex unit, both palms flat against the plaster, and inched my way to the big bush at the corner of the unit. The textured plaster scraped my skin like sandpaper. I stepped in and out and over and between planted tulips, flowers and assorted stones ringing the flower bed.

Chewy still hadn't moved. I was beginning to feel simultaneously like a genius and a complete idiot.

Then I heard two kids come walking down West Morris, playing rap music. They were laughing and shouting but I couldn't make out at what. I pushed myself deeper into the bush and flatter against the plaster wall of the duplex unit. Then the kids' voices faded away and I stuck my fingers into the bush, trying to see if Chewy was still there and if he was looking my way.

He was and he wasn't looking my way.

This is it, I thought.

I jumped out from behind the bush as fast as I could and at the same time tried to look nonchalant, casually walking to the corner directly opposite Chewy. But he didn't bark. Chewy didn't jump, he didn't move; he didn't even give me any sign in his body language that he recognised who I was. He just looked at me, then through me and then away.

For me, that was a big disappointment but before anything could change I walked across the street and put the leash on him without giving him a chance to think. And he let me do so. Then, when I stepped out of the street onto the corner beside him, he stood up on all fours, gently body-bumped me and stood ready to go home.

I said all those little endearments you would to a dog you loved in that kind of a situation: 'Chewy, Chewy, so glad to find you', 'Oh, I love you, my little sweetie', 'You gave us quite a fright!', 'Have you had enough of your big adventure again?' and so forth.

And then we went home.

Who knows how long Chewy sat at the corner on West Morris Avenue? Was he there most of the time? Maybe he was in some kind of Zen-like trance, sitting there on the corner, watching the traffic. Was he confused and not sure what to do next? Perhaps he was waiting for the traffic to thin so that he could cross the street and walk home? Or had he heard me and gone to the corner to wait? Did he know he'd lost his sense of crossing traffic safely?

I'll never know. The important thing is he made it home safely, again.

Chapter Twenty-Five
Massage Therapy? On a Dog?

'Just shoot me.'

That's my knee-jerk response to the touchy-feely psychology movement, magic crystals, astrology and all the rest of the New Age, alternative and pseudo-science movements ushered in by the Age of Aquarius.

Line me up with evidence-based medicine, quack watch, consumer reports and ConsumerLab, *The New York Times Review of Books*, Seymour Hersh's reporting, Bill Moyer's *Journal* and *Sixty Minutes*. So, I was about to vomit when one of our neighbours who spotted Chewy limping suggested massage – she had noticed his right leg seemed stiff when he got up. He hobbled on it a bit. Limping, she called it.

'What?'

'Yes, I gave our dog a massage. She loved it and I think it extended her life.'

Her dog had lived an extra six months, she reported.

Spare me, I thought. But I noticed Chewy was limping: she was right. Then guilt set in. At times I'm embarrassingly judgemental and dismissive, sometimes quite unfairly, while Lauren is quite the opposite. So one day, while Lauren was at work, I thought, looking at Chewy, limping around the kitchen: *Why not? What can it hurt, except my pride, if proved wrong?* If dog massages actually improved Chewy's life, I'd stand corrected.

It took me about a week debating with myself to get over my disdain for 'touchy-feely approaches'. Then some time to get over what might be called my resentment, should I be proved wrong. Plus my ego, or pride, because I'd have to tell the neighbour she was right: massages actually worked on dogs.

A week of research followed. The local library had massage books and YouTube videos on how to massage your dog. I watched several videos, picking what appeared to be the most professional presentation. Then I collected ideas from library books and checked out the local bookstores. Following this I planned an approach to start the massage with a skittish Chewy.

The idea was to start slowly, rubbing his head and ears, and see how he responded. If Chewy allowed me to rub him then I would continue moving down the rest of his body until I reached the base of his spine and his right leg. Those were the areas that were the most painful.

While Lauren and I watched a movie and Chewy was sprawled out on the floor, I began.

'Chewy,' I called.

He didn't get up immediately. Lying in front of the couch before the TV, his head turned towards me but his body didn't move. *Not a good sign*, I thought.

I got off the couch and gently laid my hands on his shoulders. He looked at me, puzzled. Then I remembered my plan: start with his ears and head.

Slowly I scratched his head and then massaged his ears, stroking them in unison with my thumb on top, fingers moving lightly, touching his underside. No startled response. He cocked his head to the left as if he wanted me to scratch just below his right ear. So I did. Then he leaned right and forwards as if he wanted me to scratch down around the back of his neck, just above the shoulders. So I did. Then I gently pushed my thumbs and pads of my hands away and down his shoulders – I was surprised at how muscular his shoulders were.

Gently but firmly, I massaged them. Chewy spun his head around and looked at me with an expression that seemed to say, 'What are you doing?' But he didn't pull away or attempt to get up. Working down the curve of his spine, I expected him to get up and pull away at any moment, but he didn't. When I got close to his tail, he did pull away. *Enough for one day*, I thought.

Apparently Chewy had the same thought. Unaccustomed to that intimate a human touch, he got up and moved closer to Lauren. When he had settled at her feet, he looked over at me. I don't know how to describe his look: it was a steady but short gaze, intense but brief, quickly staring at me with disdain as if I was some alien creature. He looked away.

I had no idea if he liked the touching. Maybe it was just the fact that this was something new and Chewy did not know how to react or what to think.

Several days later he came into my studio. He looked at me, paintbrush in hand, my face partially streaked with paint. I probably looked nuts in my paint-splattered work overalls, wool cap pulled down over my balding head, my large ears sticking out and wearing old tennis shoes in tatters.

'Oh hi, Chewy,' I said, pleased that he'd come in to visit.

He glanced up at me and spun his body around so his head faced the door, his back to me and lay down. Nothing said, no touching – just my dog lying down on a mat facing the door and content merely to be there for now. We enjoyed each other's silent company for several hours: a silent companionship.

For the first hour, I looked over at him every few minutes to see if he was still there: he was. While I painted, he snoozed or kept a silent guard near the door. Whatever was going on, I wanted him to stay so I left him alone. Every so often I snuck glances at him, watching his fur rise with each breath, his head over his paws and his tail wrapped around his body. I viewed these visits from Chewy as special – maybe Elizabeth Marshall Thomas was right when she said in *The Hidden Life of Dogs* that a part of what they want is just to 'be' in their pack with other dogs. Maybe we were forming a pack, the Klein pack.

In the next few weeks, I repeated my fledgling massages. At the front door before going on a walk, I gave Chewy a few rubs to his head. While we were watching a movie before the TV, he received a gentler stroking of his ears. In the kitchen when we were waiting for his food to be laid out by Lauren, he rubbed his head against my thigh. I rubbed back.

Several more times he came into my studio.

And then it happened.

One Saturday night while we were eating pizza and watching a Hollywood blockbuster, all of us, Lauren, Chewy and me in front of the TV, I felt a nudge at my thigh. With a pizza slice in hand, halfway to my mouth, I looked down. Chewy had got up from his usual spot on the floor, walked over and nudged me. He nudged me again.

I turned slightly in my seat, bringing my knees around to the right just enough to face him. When I looked down again, Chewy stretched his neck forwards and up, laying his head gently on my thighs, just above the knees.

All without making eye contact.

For reasons I'll never be able to explain, I took this as a sign that he wanted a massage. He didn't back away as I bit off a large chunk of pizza, put the rest of the slice down and then began massaging delicately between his ears and down his neck, pizza dangling from my mouth.

He breathed out and relaxed.

Before I realised it, I had two hands on him, giving him a mini-massage down his spine. I opened my legs, pushed my chair back a few inches and repositioned myself, fully expecting him to lay his head back on my knees. But he didn't: he pulled out and slipped sideways in front of my body. Now Chewy turned his body and stepped forwards a tad so that I could massage further down his spine and back. Surprised, I said: 'Oh, you like it now?'

He didn't respond but simply waited for my laying-on of hands. I worked over his spine and hind legs, gently cupping my fingers around his back legs and smoothing his fur down as I ran my hand down each leg and over his paws. When I sought to start again at the top of his spine, he gingerly pulled away. His wagging tail I took as a sign he liked it, but was done. I don't think Lauren was aware of what had happened as she was transfixed by the movie and whatever paper project she was working on. Chewy simply walked back around the table where I was eating and lay down before the TV screen with its surround sound booming.

Of course I was elated. When I told Lauren she said, 'Oh, that's nice, really nice,' between pizza bites and Tom Cruise fighting aliens in the recent remake of H.G. Wells' *The War of the Worlds*.

That night I slept soundly.

* * *

Slowly, Chewy was accepting something like a massage. My goal was to have him lie down on his side and allow me to give him a full body massage, which might not be possible. Running my hand gently over his paws I found he pulled his feet up and backed out of my hand. When I stroked down his spine as I came to his hip socket he pulled away – he was particularly sensitive on his right hip. Something was going on there. But he did come up for a massage around his head, below his jaw and under and around his collar.

'You like that?' I asked. He had one of two responses: either he leaned into the scratching or gentle massaging, softly growling, or he rubbed his muzzle against my leg, shaking his head in short little bursts and emitting a low growl. Then he'd begin to nip and bite almost as if in play. If I began a soft rough housing with him, Chewy would become more vigorous, pulling, growling and chewing on my fingers and knuckles.

I could grab his large incisors and pull on them and he would resist, growling and pulling. Or suddenly he would rush forwards and nip at my thighs.

'What are those bruise marks on your inner thigh?' Lauren asked me late one evening when I was changing into my pyjamas. I looked down.

'Wow, I don't know!' I said in disbelief. There were half-inch long, blue and purple bruises along my inner thigh. They looked suspiciously like bite marks.

'Where did they come from? I don't remember bumping anything.'

'Oh, I bet it's Chewy,' Lauren said, pulling the blankets over her shoulders. Before I could answer she was deep into reading her mystery novel. She turned to me and said, 'Your turn to get the lights.'

The rule is, last one in bed has to turn off the lights: she had outfoxed me again. In the darkness, I tried to think of when or how Chewy might have given me bruises. The next morning while shaving it dawned on me: 'It's the rough-house playing with Chewy,' I said.

'What are you talking about?' Lauren asked, turning to me as she was getting ready for work.

'It's his little nips that almost break the skin,' I explained, 'when we rough house, Chewy and I. That's where the bruises came from.'

I've got to be more careful, I told myself.

'Yes, Sherlock,' Lauren said. 'But what about *my* bruises?'

I had no quick answer. Anyway, I stopped thinking about it because I didn't want to cut myself shaving.

* * *

Chewy's sensitivity when I gave him a massage made us pay more attention to his limp. We noticed how he often limped when he got up to walk after he'd been lying down. And we'd often wondered why, when he played so joyously with other dogs, he would suddenly quit rough housing and go and lay down by himself in the sand.

'Go play with your buddies,' Lauren would suggest. Chewy, panting rapidly, paws in front of him, body stretched out in the sand, would turn his head to look at Lauren and then turn away as if nothing had registered. Perhaps he was thinking: 'You go play, I'm tired. I got pain in my hip. The soft sand helps, boss.'

Sitting on the grass across from Chewy, Lauren and I would just be befuddled. Warm sunlight, fresh air, open space and a lot of dogs to play with and Chewy just walked away and sat down? Why? We decided to get him X-rayed.

'I think it's just a matter of time...'

Our vet Mike explained to Lauren and me what he could see when reviewing Chewy's X-rays. Mike pointed out where there was arthritis in Chewy's right hip and along his spine. He thought it likely that at some point after Chewy's hip plates had stopped growing, when he was a year or perhaps a little older, he had had some trauma to his right hip. It might have been a major automobile accident, which could have broken some of the supportive structures in Chewy's right hip. When Chewy was recovering from that accident, the healing process calcified back over, thicker than the same bone structure in his left hip. The major accident, or perhaps several small ones, meant his right femur head was less deeply cradled in the hip socket than normal.

This accounted for Chewy's stiffness. When he first got up from lying down he moved stiffly in his back quarters, particularly his right leg. He dragged the leg for a bit, barely putting any weight on it. You could see in his left paw how his toes were more deeply splayed because of the uneven weight distribution. His thigh muscles in his left leg were also more developed, as Chewy placed more weight on this leg to compensate for the pain in his right hip.

It was another mystery about Chewy's time on the streets: it's not surprising that it appears he was hit by a car – living on the streets for a year or so he was at risk. He must have healed himself. Chewy must have found a safe spot and laid low while his body healed. How did he eat or take care of the necessities of life during those healing processes? We don't know but he found a way to survive.

What was surprising was that he was fully grown when it happened. When we first got Chewy off the streets, Mike thought he was a year and a half old. Did that mean Chewy had been hit by a car then healed just a few months before Cecelia, Lauren and I came into his life? Is that why he moved over near the canal and Gary's house? Lauren and I had noticed when feeding him near Gary's house that when Chewy moved, often his back legs appeared stiff. We thought then he most likely had arthritis.

That all made sense: sometimes when I massaged Chewy and touched his right leg where he was probably struck by a car, he pulled away. Now, I knew why.

Chapter Twenty-Six
A Handful of Angels

Recently, when Cecelia closed her front door to run errands, stepping out into the shade of her front porch, she had seen the long-haired, reddish-brown dog walking down the sidewalk.

It was Labor Day, a hot Modesto holiday. The thermometer outside read 102 degrees.

The dog walked fast, head down, sniffing back and forth, drop-shouldered and tail down.

He's hot, and lost, Cecelia thought, *and confused*. She ran back into her house, slid her bag off her shoulder, down onto the couch. When she rushed back outside, the dog was gone.

I'm too slow, Cecelia thought, *already he's gone*. Cecelia's house is located on the corner of two streets. Quickly, she walked down the side of her house, looking up and down Achor Court for the dog. He'd vanished.

Ten minutes later Cecelia heard a knock on her front door. When she opened it, Ellen her neighbour smiled and asked, 'Did you see that dog?'

Ellen lived a block and a half away in a corner house on West Morris Avenue. In her early fifties, hair tied in a ponytail, she'd watched the dog circling by her house.

He's lost, she thought, *probably frightened and hungry.*

'He looks exhausted! What are we going to do?' Ellen exclaimed.

Standing on her front porch, Cecelia didn't hesitate.

'Well, let's go get him,' she said, grabbing her house keys and pulling her front door shut.

Achor Court is a narrow street. On the north side of the street, backyards face the irrigation canal – the same canal Chewy had called home. As Cecelia and Ellen walked down the street they saw their neighbours outside in their yards or heard them barbecuing in their backyards. Passing John's house, he waved as he washed his classic VW station wagon.

Up the street, on the corner of Magnolia Avenue and Achor Court, Cecelia spotted the dog walking down the middle of Magnolia Avenue towards busy West Morris Avenue. She ran up the sidewalk in front of him to turn him around, away from the traffic.

'Shoo, go back!' Cecelia shouted in the middle of the street, waving her arms up and down. 'Go on,' she yelled in a gentler tone, 'get outta here!'

Cecelia stomped her left foot hard on the asphalt but it made no sound. She picked up a stick to scratch and thump on the street.

It frightened the dog. With Cecelia gyrating in the middle of the street, the dog turned around. He scampered towards the canal.

Ellen, talking to John, saw the dog run towards the canal embankment and the footbridge. 'That's him,' she said.

Cecelia came running down Magnolia Avenue. She yelled, 'Come on, you guys, come and help me with this dog!'

Her yell wasn't a request. She barked her demand like a drill sergeant chastising fresh recruits.

Ellen and John, galvanised into action, ran towards Cecelia and the poor dog.

At the canal footbridge, the dog turned left towards Sycamore Avenue. He went along the near side of the canal bank, running and stopping to see if Cecelia was following him.

When Cecelia saw him looking at her, she knew there was only one thing to do: she took off running. She ran across the footbridge, up along the northern side of the canal towards Sycamore Avenue. The idea, once again, was to try and head the dog off before he reached the busier street.

Her flip-flops didn't fly off as she high-kicked it along the canal bank. Dust billowed up. After twenty feet, Cecelia was winded. With each breath she felt pain in her side, pain under her ribs.

As she reached Sycamore Avenue a U-Haul truck rambled fast across the two-lane Sycamore Bridge. The down draft blew hot air against her blouse and hair but luckily she got across before the dog arrived.

She turned to go back down the canal. The dog paused to look up at this seventy-one-year-old woman facing him. Cecelia was panting, her forehead sweaty from running, her grey hair wind-blown, her body bent down and both her arms reaching out to the dog.

'Here, honey. Here, my little sweetie,' Cecelia cooed.

Cecelia's plan was to walk towards the dog, reassure him and get a leash around him. There was only one problem: Cecelia didn't have a leash and the dog did not have a collar on. Ellen and John didn't have a leash. Everyone forgot about getting a leash; they just reacted to the situation, afraid they would lose the dog.

By this time, two other neighbours, a man and a woman, had joined the group. Both lived near the canal and had noticed the action with the stray dog. Curiously, they walked over to the canal embankment to see what was happening and to offer help. Cecelia yelled over to them, 'Do either of you have a dog leash? We are going to need one in order to help this poor guy!' The woman ran off to her house to retrieve one.

In the meantime Ellen and John had not crossed the footbridge. They'd come up behind the dog. This meant he was now caught in the middle, with Cecelia on one side and Ellen and John on the other. The male neighbour, closer to Cecelia, was watching.

The dog turned away from Cecelia and ran, alarmed, a short way back along the canal bank. That's when he saw Ellen and John, smiling and walking towards him. John was silent and slightly behind Ellen, towering over her. Ellen leaned forward as if to catch the dog. Then they both stopped, their eyes widened and their mouths dropped open.

Totally panicked and gathering speed, the dog ran in a slight diagonal straight towards Ellen and John. Then he turned and leapt.

Cecelia yelled, 'Oh, no!' and threw her hands up. Ellen and John gasped.

We've all seen leaps in movies: kids racing and jumping off stone quarry cliffs into their favourite swimming hole, their slow-motion bodies falling in through the air, arms waving, legs kicking, yelling 'Geronimo!' and ending with a gigantic splash. Or in some exotic vacation island advertisement, a native diving off a fifty-foot cliff for tourists and falling in a graceful, arched, slow motion, beautiful swan dive.

When an older, panicked and confused long-haired dog jumps into a canal on a hot Labor Day afternoon, the leap isn't graceful or beautiful, nor is it in slow motion. Rather, he makes a kind of a pathetic flop, a cross between a hard belly flop and a splat. Everybody watching winced when he hit the water.

Ugh, John said to himself, *I bet that hurt*!

The canal was full of water, four feet deep. Cold water from the High Sierras filled the canal, as well as run-off from fertilisers and the garbage thrown in. Other more dangerous items such as bicycles, shopping trollies, broken glass, broken tree limbs and tyres also floated in the canal water. Who knew what else?

On hitting the water the current spun the dog sideways and then tail-and-rear-first, he went down the canal. Immediately the dog began to swim, or tried to swim. At first, he tried to walk on the water, lifting his paws high as if trying to lift himself out of the water. The current spun him like a cork.

Within minutes he was carried ten feet downstream towards the low Sycamore Bridge. Fighting hard, the dog paddled diagonally across the water flow but every time he tried to climb out of the canal, he did not have the strength to pull himself from the water. He would scramble up the canal bank six or seven inches and then fall back again into the current.

From his struggles Cecelia could see he was lame in his left leg. Each time he struggled, he fell back further down the canal and deeper into the water. His mouth and eyes were barely above water. After two more attempts, his eyes caught Cecelia's.

They looked at each other. She knew he had given up.

Cecelia did not think, she acted: immediately she threw both her arms out straight like airplane wings and started walking down the sloped canal embankment, her eyes still on the dog. Their eyes met again.

She knew she had to get this dog: he was about to drown.

Later, when asked what she was thinking, Cecelia knew she wasn't thinking at all. She didn't feel the coldness of the water or the green slime along the canal bottom; she couldn't feel whether or not her flip-flops stayed on her feet. She didn't think about whether her freshly-ironed Capri pants or beautiful, loose-fitting knit shirt would get stained with green gook or muddy patches, she just could not watch the dog drown.

As she got closer to the bottom of the canal she was almost sliding down the embankment slope. The shock of what she had done was over; she was just focused on trying to save the dog. She kept her eyes on the dog and placed herself in the path of the current so that he would float into her arms.

The dog floating, bobbing, struggling to keep his head above water and failing, then resurfacing with long red hair plastered against his skull, paws kicking and splashing in the current, bumped into Cecelia's outstretched arms. She wrapped her arms around his struggling body and held on.

Dry, the dog weighed eighty-five pounds. Wet, frightened and struggling against her body, he felt like an iron anchor, a dead-weighted stone. Cecelia's feet slipped in the muddy canal bottom, her weight shifting and wobbly, as she tried to hold the struggling dog against her chest. The water surge threatened to suck them both under. She pushed her chest against the current but Cecelia could feel herself and the dog being pulled along by it. She was surprised it was as strong as it was – when standing on the canal bank there did not appear to be much of a current at all.

Cecelia's flip-flops slipped again and again on the bottom. *Where are my feet? What am I stepping on? Why won't this dog hold still?* she wondered. Cecelia pulled him tighter against her chest. 'It's OK, honey, it's OK,' she murmured. But she wasn't sure the dog was OK.

Cecelia started paying attention to the fact they were moving closer to the street bridge. When the canal is full, there is not much head clearance between the top of the water and the underside of the bridge. If she slipped, they'd go under it and she knew they would be underwater when passing beneath the road. Who knew what lurked under there to block their path? And how long could she hold her breath underwater? What would this poor scared dog do? She knew they had to get out of the water and get out now.

Chest deep in water, Cecelia pushed against the current, the dog up flat against her body. *How can I walk up the canal embankment with this dog in my arms?* she wondered. *The dog is too heavy, the water current too strong and the surface too slippery.*

She looked towards the embankment. Four neighbours standing there were watching the drama unfold.

One had a leash. Carefully, the male neighbour began stepping down the steep embankment to help. John started moving too.

Without thinking, Cecelia looked up at them and yelled, 'John, get in here!' Again, this was not a request.

And that's exactly what happened. John walked down the canal embankment into the water next to Cecelia. His arms steadied her. In unison they walked towards the side, where the female neighbour edged over the canal embankment to dangle the leash for Cecelia and John to grab.

Since the dog did not have a collar on they had to loop the leash around his neck to create a collar and leash. Easier said than done when you're in moving water, trying to hold an eighty-five-pound dog safely. Several times Cecelia and John struggled to get the leash around the dog's neck while staying upright in the slimy canal. Fumbling, they finally did it.

They fought the current by walking backwards against it and diagonally across the width of it towards the north side. Cecelia still balanced the dog in her arms.

The other male neighbour had crossed over to the north side of the canal embankment to help. He then partially walked down the embankment towards the water-logged trio, grabbing at the end of the dog's leash. John turned and lifted the leash higher. After several attempts the man grabbed hold of the leash and began pulling the dog up the slope of the embankment.

Worried the dog might choke, Cecelia asked the man to be gentle. It would not do to strangle the dog in the process of trying to save him. But when he had the leash safely and securely, John and Cecelia were then able to turn around and search underwater for the dog's rear end. 'Here it is,' John said, smiling.

Cecelia pushed the dog's rear up the cement embankment as the man pulled.

Struggling, the dog allowed himself to be pulled and shoved up until his four paws found traction. Then he tried to scramble up the embankment. The dog's lame leg collapsed under his body. His eyes rolled wild with fear and exhaustion.

John caught the dog as he started to slide back down into the canal. When they finally pushed and pulled the dog out of the canal to safety, the leash was passed to the woman. The male neighbour turned and gave his hand to help John out of the water. Both of them then reached down for one of Cecelia's hands. Slippery but safe, they pulled Cecelia out, like a ship being raised, water dripping off her arms and clothes.

Within minutes everyone was up the embankment. Cecelia's legs and Capri pants were green with canal slime; John's jeans were soaked. The dripping dog looked like a mop with four slimy, skinny wet sticks poked into it.

Then the dog began to shake himself dry.

Everyone stepped back, yelling, 'Yeah!'

The dog lay on the embankment, exhausted. Cecelia worried that they might have hurt him and crouched down to examine him. He looked lame in one leg, wet but dehydrated, and quite old. Then the woman who brought the leash ran to her house and got a bowl of water. The dog lapped it up.

Cecelia watched him struggle to his feet and drink. Her wet clothes, now coated with dust from scuffling around with the dog, hung on her like wet laundry put out to dry. Cecelia focused on the dog's welfare. Was he OK? Had he hurt his lame leg? How was he breathing? Focusing all her nursing skills on her new rescue, she failed to notice John and the other male neighbour walking home, having done their part.

Ellen and the female neighbour stayed with Cecelia and the dog on the canal embankment. What were they going to do next? The three women stood looking at each other, wondering what to do. It was hot and the dog almost certainly needed medical attention.

A single lane road parallels the north side of the canal. The lane is only two blocks long and dead ends at Sycamore Avenue. Three women standing beside a bridge, one of them soaking wet, the others holding onto a shaking dog, demands an explanation.

A man driving a truck with a camper shell stopped in the road. Leaning out of the window, he yelled, 'Are you ladies in trouble? Do you need some help?' He was clean-shaven, with a broad smile and near their age.

Ellen looked at him and immediately said, 'Yes, this old dog was lost in the neighbourhood and he needed help. She,' Ellen said, pointing to Cecelia, 'she jumped into the canal to save him.'

'Oh, jeez,' the man said, 'wait a moment!' He drove his truck off the road and up onto the embankment. Then he parked next to the dog so the shadow of his truck would provide shade for him.

'Heat exhaustion,' he explained, stepping out of the truck. 'It's so hot, you got to watch out for heat exhaustion.'

They heard the sounds of an automatic garage door opening. Cecelia looked around the parked truck. Just then, another neighbour behind them opened her garage and shouted, 'Do you need help? I heard all the ruckus and wanted to check.'

'A little water would help,' Cecelia said. She sat down on the running board of the truck, her clothes dusty but drying in the hot sun. The woman graciously brought cold water for all of them and another bowl of water for the dog.

Cecelia's mind was racing: she knew they needed to get the dog some medical attention. A veterinarian should check his vital signs and lame leg for injury. The canal water was probably full of chemicals – his bobbing head must have swallowed lots of this polluted water.

She saw the truck driver had a mobile phone in his pocket.

'Could you make a call to 911?' she asked.

As he made the call, Cecelia could hear the 911 operator asking specific questions about the incident. Cecelia then gestured for the phone. 'We just pulled a dog out of the canal and we need help,' she said.

'We can't help you,' responded the 911 dispatcher.

'What?' Cecelia asked, shocked by the dispatcher's response.

'There is no city animal officer on duty right now.'

Upset, Cecelia said, 'My neighbour across the street is a police officer and if he were home, he would be helping us right now.'

'Oh,' the 911 dispatcher responded. 'Well, we can try sending a county animal control officer to help, not a city officer but someone from the Animal Control facility.'

After ending the call, the waiting began on that hot afternoon. Everyone sat under the shade of the truck along the canal embankment, waiting for the animal control officer to arrive. After half an hour, Ellen got impatient. 'I don't think they are coming.'

She got up and began walking around. The man driving the truck grew worried that he might get a ticket because his truck was parked up on the canal embankment by the bridge where a passing police car could see it, or someone could call in a complaint. He was concerned he'd had his truck there too long and it was illegal.

Finally, Ellen walked out onto Sycamore Avenue to glance right and left down the street for the Animal

Control truck. A blue car driving down the street stopped after noticing Ellen standing in the middle of the street, squinting apparently and looking like she needed help.

'Yes,' was Ellen's response. She repeated the story that she had told to the man driving the truck with the camper shell. Again, explaining how this stray dog needed help and Cecelia had jumped in the canal to save the dog.

The man responded by parking his car. He explained that his wife was the board president of one of the local animal rescue non-profit organisations. Then he walked over with Ellen to see the dog lying in the shade of the pick-up truck and to talk to the rest of the group. After introductions, he said, 'Look, I think my wife and I can help but I need to go pick her up across town. We'll be back, I promise you.'

Cecelia sat, sweating and dirty.

Ellen and the truck driver discussed whether or not the man in the blue car would come back, let alone bring his wife. But he did. And he did bring his wife.

They came prepared. The wife brought blankets, a leash, water and food for the dog. After he'd eaten, they placed the dog in the back seat of their car.

'Here's my name and phone number,' Cecelia said. 'You two are angels.'

They all exchanged addresses, names and phone

numbers. The Animal Control officer never showed up, but the couple did take the dog to the vet the next day.

* * *

There were no apparent injuries to the dog from jumping into the canal (there weren't for John or Cecelia either). The vet said the dog apparently wasn't used to a leash. He wondered if the dog had always been a stray since his behaviour indicated a poorly-socialised dog. It was unusual for a dog as old as this never to have been leash trained.

After the vet cleared him, the couple took the dog home and named him Ivan. A few days later, when Cecelia called to check up on them and Ivan's condition, the wife answered.

'Oh,' she said. 'My husband never stops for stray animals. Every time I bring a new dog home, he says, "Oh no, not another dog!" Why he stopped and was willing to take Ivan home, I'll never know. Ivan has become my husband's dog. He has integrated well into his new home, getting along with our other dogs. It's a small miracle.'

Cecelia thinks the husband was Ivan's angel. Lauren and I believe Cecelia is Ivan's angel as well as Chewy's angel. Maybe Ivan has two angels, his new dad and Cecelia.

I don't believe in angels, but I believe in people. People like Cecelia, my wife, Denise, Rob, Gary, John, Ellen, Patty and Bob, and the countless others in our neighbourhood who helped feed, shelter and rescue our dog.

Most of all, I believe in Chewy.

Chapter Twenty-Seven
The Mystery of Chewy's DNA

After we'd had Chewy X-rayed, and discovered he'd suffered a trauma such as a car injury, we started wondering about his dog ancestry. Lauren and I had thought Chewy was most likely a mix of Saint Bernard, Border collie or collie. I thought the Saint Bernard was a no-brainer, really obvious. The other guesses I didn't have a clue about, except that a Collie made sense to me given Chewy's coat, but we could see his head was not shaped in the blocky shape of a Saint Bernard's.

Given that I'm a tad obsessive, I went to the public library and checked out dog breed picture books. My foolish assumption was that I might discover a picture that came close to matching Chewy. Of course, nothing like that happened.

I asked Donna, our dog trainer, to give us her best guess on Chewy's ancestry and we liked her approach. We were in our living room. Chewy was between the chair and sofa in front of the TV, with the afternoon light on his red fur. He looked resplendent.

'Well,' Donna said, 'look at his ears. Chewy has a triangular drop ear. Saint Bernard ears are large and floppy – Chewy's ears remind me of the Australian Shepherd breed.' Then she stepped back and squinted, her eyes looking down at Chewy's chest to his paws (apparently to the trained eye they reveal something). Donna impressed me with the kind of analytic approach she had to accessing his ancestry, checking each body part. She continued, saying, 'He does not have Saint Bernard eyes either but he does have a nice round foot. Saint Bernards have a cat foot, with a big round shape.'

Lauren and I were both fascinated. She walked around Chewy like someone accessing a horse or sculpture, leaning back, looking at him from the side and from end to end, and then straight on again, frontally.

Her opinion was actually quite close to what Mike suggested: a mountain dog mix with Australian shepherd or collie. Mike also suggested Chewy might have some chow chow in him.

Lauren and I thought that was accurate, no question. I was particularly impressed by the way both of them picked out specific features of ears, eyes, eyebrows, fluffy tail type, the way Chewy held his tail, as well as his fluffy pantaloons, and the fur down his four legs. Donna and Mike made other observations about his teeth and mouth. They had me convinced of their reasoning as to their choice of breeds from behaviour and specific body parts.

Then I surfed the Web. I discovered we could do a DNA test on Chewy. The results would be relative to the state of science at the time and both our vet and dog trainer didn't have much trust in their accuracy. Still, we picked out one company, paid their fee and received in the mail an envelope with swab sticks for saliva samples.

The first attempt at getting saliva from Chewy did not work out well. Of course he was not the least interested. When Lauren put the swabs in Chewy's cheeks to obtain the saliva amount recommended by the instructions, he bit them. She sent them off to the company anyway, hoping it would work. Of course, it didn't – the first try didn't contain enough of a sample. We got an email alerting us to the fact that another envelope was in the mail for a second swipe.

After the second envelope came, Chewy had an appointment to get his teeth cleaned. There was plaque built up on his teeth. Lauren thought it would be convenient to have Mike obtain the saliva samples while Chewy was out for his teeth-cleaning procedure. Graciously he agreed to do so; he was also curious about the results. Mike's staff then sent off Chewy's second sample.

Several weeks later, via email, we got our results.

* * *

Of course, you can guess what happened when we got the DNA analysis back. The *Wisdom Panel* report provided the results overleaf.

The Mystery of Chewy's DNA

The company's database included DNA markers from over 200 dog breeds, a total of 321 markers. Using complex maths and computer models, Chewy's DNA was sorted and combined into millions of different ancestral tree lines until the most probable ones emerged. Those results used 92% of Chewy's DNA, 75% of which matched pure bred DNA, with the remaining 25% matching mixed breed DNA. Chewy's second swab tested well.

The test results predicted Chewy was a Chinese Shar-Pei mix, Rhodesian ridgeback, chow chow and toy fox terrier cross. The report provided to us stated one of Chewy's parents was a mixture of chow chow/Rhodesian ridgeback/toy fox terrier cross. The other parent was a Chinese Shar-Pei Mix.

At first, this result made no sense to me – I'd preferred our guess that Chewy was a Border collie, collie and Saint Bernard mix. My first impulse was to dismiss the DNA results. Then I decided to call Mike and Donna to get their response. Maybe they'd help me understand them. I also called the company.

The company was incredibly helpful. For each body part I asked about, they provided, based on their DNA analysis, the likely source of each trait. Chewy's reddish and light cream colour fur was most likely carried by all four breeds they identified. His black-tipped hairs, a sable trait, more than likely came from the Chinese Shar-Pei or his mixed-breed genetics.

The black on his muzzle is carried by the Shar-Pei, the chow chow or the Rhodesian ridgeback. Chewy's white hair probably came from the toy fox terrier or the mixed breed genes. His long coat similarly came from the mixed-breed influence or the chow chow. Feathering on his legs, tail and ears might have come from the chow chow or the mixed-breed genes also.

Chewy's ears which fold over are influenced by all four breeds. His muzzle length and brow width are a combination of the four breeds.

This information came almost verbatim from the company's DNA report. There didn't seem to be any Saint Bernard influence, just an odd collection of genes that led to Chewy's distinctive look. Their analysis and explanation did seem plausible. We decided, perhaps when a new gold standard in dog DNA analysis had definitely been established, that we would test Chewy's DNA again. For now, the current results were one more set of facts that help explain the wonderful dog we loved.

* * *

As Emma, our other dog, got much older, Chewy started to assert himself: he challenged her on who entered the back door first. He also insisted that he could pick which dog bed he wanted to sleep on. In these small ways he'd begun to challenge her dominance. Two years after

Chewy joined our household Emma died; he helped fill her place.

I hated Emma's death. I'd never euthanised a dog before, let alone watch one I loved die before my eyes. Lauren had. For me, putting her down somehow broke a trust, while for Lauren, euthanising Emma was a final necessary act of kindness.

I understood the necessity and the kindness of it, even agreed with it. But my emotions were just too raw.

Chewy must have smelt death growing on Emma, but he didn't get upset or treat her any differently – Emma and Chewy weren't close. As Emma weakened, Chewy grew from adolescence to young adulthood.

With the cats he renegotiated who was boss. When I picked Fred up out of Chewy's way so he could enter the back door to get his dinner, often he would brush my leg as he passed me. When it looked like Pip was about to swat Chewy for no other reason than to keep him in his place, Lauren shooed Pip away. Chewy often just looked at her but other times, he brushed up against her affectionately as he walked by her, too.

In tiny and small ways like these we earned Chewy's trust; it took a long time.

Sniff walks where Chewy got more freedom, and massages where he could control the degree and places of touching, furthered that trust. Daily walks and visits to the doggie park helped enormously.

A grassroots organisation of the local dog community and veterinarians built the doggie park two years after we rescued Chewy. It sits right by Gary's house and Chewy loves it. Imagine half a city block swarming with dogs. Well, not literally swarming, but a large half-long city block lot fenced for dogs. Imagine the moment Chewy sets his paws outside our front door, he can smell the doggie park and the dogs in the park.

One of Chewy's walking routes now goes directly to the doggie park. Trotting down Magnolia Avenue, approaching the crosswalk at West Morris Avenue, Chewy suddenly, a few feet before the crosswalk, drops behind Lauren and swings over to her right side. Then he does a brisk, forceful left turn in front of and across her legs, pulling her right arm holding the leash sharply to the left, directly towards the doggie park. There's no mistaking where he wants to go. Effectively and efficiently, he's spun Lauren around and pulls her towards the park, like a husky team in the Iditarod sled race.

'Look at this,' Lauren says, smiling. She's halfway across the street by the time I look; I smile.

'Honestly.'

She continues feigning exasperation at my having instilled free choice in Chewy's head. The closer we get to the doggie park, the stronger he pulls.

The park itself is filled with dogs flinging themselves at each other: sniffing, play barking, bowing, rolling on their backs, running in great circles or along the fence chasing each other. From the sidelines the owners watch, alert to any aggressive behaviour.

Chewy sniffs any dog coming up to greet him. Typically, he leaps and sprints onto the grassy and sand-filled play area. Overtly aggressive dogs he avoids. Occasionally he runs along the fence, playing chase. More often he searches out youthful adolescent energy, still bundles of wiggly puppy energy.

The galloping then begins, heads and teeth flying up in the air, chests, ears, front legs nipped and tucked until they become a surging, barking pack roaring across the field, becoming smaller and smaller till their fading yelps become lost in the shadows.

Out of nowhere they come galloping back, diving straight into their owners, clustered in lawn chairs, talking and sharing dog stories. There are screams and yells, curses and recriminations, throwing up of hands and feet as the dogs thread their way through the people's chairs, missing serious collisions by some unfathomable doggie magic.

The dogs gallop by. All the adults are yelling, some standing. Most of them are taking their seats again.

Chewy plays until his bad hip hurts and then he quietly wanders off. Or he drops his belly down into the wet sand, resting in the sun or cooling off in the shade. Whatever happens, he's happy. Whenever he becomes bored, he saunters over and nudges Lauren's fingers or thigh, telling us he's ready to leave.

Chewy had to go from his wild life on the streets to accepting a more limited lifestyle with us. While the process might never be over, great progress has been made.

Chapter Twenty-Eight
Chewy's Fan Club

'And who is this?' the grey-haired couple asked.

Chewy looked up and approached them. The woman reached out to pet him. He came forwards to let her, tail wagging.

'Oh, he's changed!' she cried.

Her husband joined in – 'Is this the same dog by the canal bridge? He was so skittish. Not anymore!' He reached down to pet him.

After Chewy entered our household and began the process of adapting to our family, Lauren took him for a walk every day. Occurrences like this happened on these walks when she met many neighbours who had tried to help Chewy. Eighty to one hundred people stopped and talked to her about how they had fed Chewy, provided water and shelter or tried to coax him into their homes to help him. She had no idea of the extent of help he'd been offered.

As Lauren and Chewy walked our neighbourhood, strangers would stop and say, 'Oh, I'm so happy to see him – he looks wonderful! We tried to get him to come home with us.'

Over and over, neighbours told us what a wonderful dog Chewy was and how they had tried to get him to come home with them. They became Chewy's fan club.

* * *

'How did you do it?' the tall thin woman in jogging shorts asked after she stopped on Virginia Avenue. 'We tried everything.'

She looked at Lauren with puzzled expectation. When Lauren explained, she said, 'Ah, progress through chemistry', and jogged on down Virginia Avenue, waving goodbye over her shoulder.

* * *

One neighbour, a middle-aged woman accompanied by her bearded husband, stopped walking to their car and instead walked down her driveway to Lauren.

'Oh, he's all grown up,' she said. 'I'd recognise him anywhere.' She then went on to tell Lauren how she'd seen Chewy running with a pack of dogs when he was a puppy. Chewy straggled behind the pack and then one day he showed up on her driveway alone. He spent the night in her front yard and driveway.

'We already had two dogs. I wanted to take him in immediately but my husband said, "Let's see if he's here in the morning. If he is, we'll take him in." Of course he wasn't.'

Chewy was gone by the time she checked on him the following morning.

She looked at her husband and then turned to Lauren. 'Good for you,' she said.

Her husband smiled.

* * *

Lauren met another woman who had seen Chewy on Roseburg Avenue. Now Roseburg Avenue is what we think of as the north-eastern boundary of Chewy's territory. The woman saw him there several times, his body wrapped around a lamp-post – the exact same behaviour he displayed wrapping his body around the telegraph pole on the canal near Gary's. Looking at Lauren, she said, 'Go figure, doesn't seem too comfortable to me to wrap your body around a pole, hugging it!'

* * *

Another neighbour who lived by Enslen School told us that on Thanksgiving Day in 2007 she looked out the window of her house. She knew Chewy was most likely huddled around his telegraph pole, hunkered down against the wind. *Oh, the poor guy*! she thought to herself. She prepared a plate of food of their holiday meal leftovers – turkey, mashed potatoes, green beans and some dog food.

'Where are you going?' her husband asked when she opened the front door with a plateful of food wrapped in aluminium foil.

She pointed down the street – 'I'm going to give that beautiful dog by the bridge a Thanksgiving meal.'

'That will be a nice holiday treat for him,' her husband said.

She walked down the street to where Chewy was huddled near the canal and gave him his own special Thanksgiving meal. I'm sure he lapped up that dinner. What an overwhelmingly generous act of giving on Thanksgiving Day – a special meal for a hobo dog from a wonderfully generous neighbour. Boy, was he lucky!

* * *

Other neighbours, Jed and Caroline, mentioned that a friend of theirs who lived in the neighbourhood would buy an extra deli sandwich at O'Brien's Market, a local grocery store. Their friend gave Chewy the extra sandwich and did this for several months in an effort to help Chewy, to try and get him off the street. Caroline mentioned her mother also tried to bring him home.

* * *

Another neighbour and his son who walked the Virginia Trail would stop every time he saw Lauren and let his son pet Chewy. The boy, about ten years old, would come running up to Chewy. 'Chewy, Chewy,' he would say, holding his hands out. 'Can I pet him?'

His dad said how nice it was to see Chewy and know that he was OK, especially since his son also cared about Chewy's welfare.

* * *

Several joggers or neighbours walking for exercise would stop and talk to Lauren when they saw her out walking Chewy. One mentioned to Lauren: 'You're our hero, you got Chewy off the street and into a safe place.'

* * *

One day, walking Chewy down Hackberry Street, a man came running out of his house. 'Is that Chewy? Oh, my goodness, you have made my day!' He came up to Lauren and looked directly at her.

'Today is my birthday. This is the best birthday present, knowing Chewy is safe and off the streets. The whole neighbourhood thanks you.' He also mentioned his wife had tried several times to bring Chewy home with her.

* * *

Later, another neighbour mentioned to Lauren that he and his wife had tried to help Chewy by befriending him and hoping they could convince him to come home with them. Like most others, Chewy outsmarted them.

* * *

One day, as Lauren and Chewy reached the Magnolia Avenue, Griswold Avenue intersection, a car stopped, hesitated and then started backing up towards them. *I wonder what is happening here*, Lauren thought to herself. The car stopped and a woman driver got out.

Lauren could hear classical music emanating from the car. 'Is that Chewy?' The woman with a gentle appearance walking towards them then said it more loudly, 'Is that Chewy?'

'Yes,' was Lauren's response, smiling as she said it.

'Oh, how wonderful it is to see him!' she said. 'My dog and I would often see Chewy on the Virginia Trail and try to help – we could never catch him.' On their walks throughout the neighbourhood, Lauren and Chewy would often see this neighbour. Most times they stopped and talked, particularly about Chewy's wellbeing.

* * *

Lauren met another young couple with their dog who saw Chewy further west, near Tully Road. They did not know him as 'Chewy' – the wife had given him another name.

* * *

There were several neighbours whose backyard faced the Virginia Trail and had known Chewy when he was living in the oleander bushes on the trail. They had also tried to help Chewy by coaxing him into their yard and house. With Chewy, street smarts and caution always trumped free food and gentle enticements.

Other neighbours who lived next to our new doggie park had seen Chewy regularly and had fed him. They lived on the other side of the canal, near Gary. The cul-de-sac by Gary's house became a giant lunch counter loaded with food, blankets and shelters for Chewy. Basically, he had a buffet table laid out before him while he lived near the bridge by the canal. Ginger and Chewy had a well-stocked pantry. We never discovered who cleaned this area up after we rescued Chewy; we assumed the well-intentioned neighbours who love dogs, and particularly Chewy, did all the hard work.

* * *

'Is that the stray dog that was living by the canal?'

While walking Chewy through the parks many homeless people asked Lauren this question – they could relate to his plight. Many were very happy he had a home and stability.

Lauren ended up befriending one homeless man. In the early part of the morning she would encounter, most days, a man walking from his sleeping spot on his way to Enslen Park. He initiated conversations by always asking about the welfare of Chewy. They began a ritual of polite checking in.

'How is Chewy this fine morning?' he would ask, to which Lauren would respond with a daily update.

When Lauren asked how he was, to her amazement and wonder, this homeless man always responded positively – 'I'm great. It's a beautiful morning and I'm doing well.'

Over the months the two of them engaged in such conversations on a regular basis. Lauren always walked away emotionally enriched, wondering how a homeless man could be so seemingly positive when she knew others who had far more than he always had plenty to complain about, yet they never seemed to act.

In the back of her mind Lauren always wondered if this homeless man hadn't at some point befriended Chewy. Lauren doesn't see this homeless man today – we don't know what became of him.

* * *

Lauren and Chewy also met Michael and Susan. Susan explained she didn't like dogs, yet she could see what a special dog Chewy was and extended herself to try and help him.

* * *

Chewy also befriended other dogs. Alice is a terrier mix of some kind who was rescued from Animal Control by her parents, Suzanne and Randy. She always appears fashionably dressed, with chokers around her neck as Suzanne, an artist, provides Alice with a wide variety of coloured chokers to choose from. Alice, Suzanne and Chewy always greet each other with enthusiasm when they meet.

* * *

We met another neighbour, Sue, who walked her giant schnauzer every day. She knew Chewy while he was on the streets and always made a point of coming over to see him when we were out on our walks.

'Chewy! It's so good to see you,' Sue would exclaim.

Lauren always had a smile on her face whenever she met a fan of Chewy's. She would walk away from these encounters feeling good about the world.

* * *

Another neighbour, Ingrid, saw Chewy when she was out walking her two dogs. 'How is that big boy, Chewy?' she would ask.

* * *

Yet another neighbour, taking advantage of the Virginia Trail by walking his two dogs, said to Lauren one day, 'Oh, there's the big red dog. He looks great! We used to see him all the time along the trail.'

* * *

Even today, six years since we received Chewy, neighbours will stop and ask how Chewy is. Most of them comment how well he looks and how he appears to be a different dog. Chewy is friendly and approaches them without being scared or timid. He allows them to pet him and at times he will extend his ritual of greeting by rubbing his head and body against them. As long as Lauren is nearby and he can keep her in eye contact, Chewy is happy to give and receive others' attention. If conversations are extended, he will lie down on the asphalt and pay attention to the world around him. Eventually, he will start looking at Lauren and moving about as if to say, 'Come on, Mom! I want to go on my walk. This is my time to explore, quit talking.' Little does he know, most of the time these conversations concern him.

Neighbours who did not know Chewy when he lived on the streets will commonly say, 'What kind of dog is he? He is beautiful!' Our standard responses are, 'He is a mutt, a true American. We thought he was part Saint Bernard, part Australian shepherd, but we had his DNA tested' – we then go on to explain the test results.

While we were working on this book, the photographer hired to take pictures of Chewy for the cover noticed all the comments he got. We were walking down the sidewalk to Graceada Park to get photos of Chewy in a natural setting. A couple riding by on their bikes saw Chewy and yelled, 'What kind of dog is that? He is handsome!'

A few minutes later, a lady walking around the park yelled over as she walked past us: 'Is that the dog who lived over by the canal?'

Then a half an hour later, after the shoot when we were walking back to our house, one of our new neighbours looked at Lauren and then Chewy before saying, 'What a beautiful dog!'

Lauren thanked her and smiled at Alisa, our photographer. 'Honestly, we didn't plan any of this!'

* * *

We know he gets attention because he is a handsome dog, but we also think Chewy's sweet energy and disposition are equally important. His beauty and personality is a child magnet: children are drawn to Chewy just as they are to many dogs. Because he is furry and handsome, lots of kids simply want to hug him like a teddy bear. Many parents will say, 'Honey, look at the cute dog!' Even better are the children who start moving their hands and arms around and immediately say, 'Doggie, doggie, I want to see the doggie!'

Several neighbours told us that school children from Enslen Grammar School fed Chewy while he lived near the bridge by the canal. When he stood by the telegraph pole greeting people, he was half a block away from the school. Parents walking their kids over the bridge to and from school every day would have walked right past him for months.

These are just some of Chewy's fan club members who have not already been mentioned in this book. There are undoubtedly more. Chewy's beauty, shyness and gentle nature endeared him to a whole community, whose hearts and minds were touched by him and who ultimately rescued him.

Epilogue

Today Chewy is a happy dog. Yes, he is confined to our house and small backyard. And yes, some days he looks bored, but he is religiously walked every day.

We always wondered if Chewy would chew our slippers, socks and furniture. We even bought him rubber dog toys that were stuffed with treats hoping he wouldn't. But he never did. They were ignored. Why he chewed Gary's slippers, earning his name, we never figured out.

On our daily 'sniff walks' Chewy chooses to visit the doggie park most days. In the doggie park, he runs free and frolics with his buddies, old and new. To see him rolling on his back in the sand, ecstatically wiggling back and forth with his mouth open, is truly heart-warming. Watching him play with his friends and steer clear of other dogs is a fascinating exercise in doggie dynamics, the rules of the temporary dog pack. Chewy loves going to the doggie park. For Lauren and me it is poignant, particularly because from there Chewy's last home on the canal bank near the bridge is within our sight – just a few hundred feet south.

Occasionally he strays from his desire to turn left and head for the doggie park. Sometimes he turns right.

When he does this, the majority of the time he is headed for Cecelia's house. Lauren and I let him decide. He turns right on West Morris Avenue and walks the two blocks, sniffing all the interesting and wonderful scents along the way. Instead of heading straight he turns left on Adams Street, walking the full block to the corner house, Cecelia's home. Sniffing up the front walkway to the front door, Chewy leads us to see the angel who saved him.

It is heart-warming when he chooses to visit Cecelia. On his sniff walks the doggie park mostly wins out but Chewy always remembers Cecelia.

Chewy and Fred still aren't the best of friends, but recently in the kitchen Chewy was eating snacks from my hand and Fred walked under Chewy's body and between his legs to get out the back door. Chewy didn't flinch, or seem uncomfortable. Fred now allows Chewy to climb over him to get into the kitchen. He also suns himself next to Chewy in the backyard without incident.

Lauren loves to garden; it helps to balance out her day job of 'living in her head'. Chewy is always with her, next to her. Right now, Lauren is in the front yard, weeding and planting; Chewy is right next to her, off-leash. Yes, *off-leash*. He stays right next to her, keeping her company.

'Lauren,' I say. She turns and looks up at me. 'He sure is your dog.'

For a moment she stares at me, puzzled, then wipes some dirt off her nose with her sleeve.

'Oh, don't give me that stuff!' she says. 'Now he is your dog too.'

And I know she is right.

* * *

Lauren and I are pretty certain had our wider neighbourhood, and the smaller group of us, not persevered in getting Chewy off the street he would probably not be alive today. Eventually, he would have been hit by a car again and hurt, or worse still, Animal Control would have eventually succeeded in catching him. Animal Control would not have had the resources or the duty to try and tame a skittish and scared dog. It's not their role to resolve behavioural issues for all of the animals that pass through their door – there are just too many animals that need help in our area.

So, feral animals and the many animals that need help must rely upon the community they live in. In the case of Chewy he had immense help from the College and Park Area neighbourhood: many recognised his need, many tried to help. We are approaching the sixth anniversary of Chewy's rescue as I write these words. Reliving that experience by writing this book reminds me of all the positive interaction shown in this community to help one dog, Chewy.

Sadly, Gary has moved to another neighbourhood. He has rescued a new dog, Red, who keeps him busy by getting into trouble regularly. We see Cecelia, Denise and Rob on a regular basis, usually when we are out walking our dogs. At eighty-four, Lauren's mom is still active and doing well, though she has had a few medical issues recently. Lauren's health is good. She believes it is a function of her mother's longevity genes. My health has remained stable.

Lauren's new mission is to find a brother or sister companion for Chewy before he gets too old. And she is persistent: she has told me part of her is waiting for the next dog to find us. We shall see if a new adventure awaits us, with Chewy helping to guide us this time.

Chewy's fan club:
Back (left to right): Gary, Cecelia, Denise and Rob
Front (left to right): Chewy, Lauren, Bruce and Fargo

Cecelia and Chewy

Lauren, Chewy and Bruce

Acknowledgements

Writing this book has been a big adventure. I love adventures – this one I got to go on with Chewy and with my wife, Lauren.

Chewy led me down alleys, across streets and into people's lives I would never have met without him. I loved it that it was mostly at the other end of his leash.

I would like to thank the *Modesto Bee*, our local newspaper, for publishing the small piece on Chewy that led Charlotte Cole to finding us.

Charlotte Cole, our editor, doubles as a detective as she was successful in finding my article about Chewy and ultimately in finding me. Her editorial comments made the book a much better read.

I would like to thank Ebury Press for seeing the merits of Chewy's story with only a book outline, a listing of chapters and one chapter written.

Initially, Chewy's behaviour bewildered me. Reading and searching the internet, I found these incredible books. Arden Moore's book, *What Dogs Want*, became the glasses through which I saw and interpreted Chewy's behaviours. I hope my descriptions don't misappropriate hers. Ted Kerasote's *Merle's Door* provided me with a model of both raising and writing about a free-thinking dog. Patricia McConnell's *The Other End of the Leash* not only advocated 'sniff walks' but her ironic title stuck in my mind – I used it several times. Elizabeth Marshall Thomas's *The Hidden Life of Dogs* suggested to me that dogs at least part of the time simply want to be with other dogs. I have tried to cite all my sources. If I have missed anyone it is unintentional.

I want to thank all our dog-loving neighbours for being interviewed for the book, as well as for their care and concern for Chewy. Special acknowledgements are in order to Cecelia French, Gary Gerhart, Denise and Rob Draizen, Barbara Parrill, Patty and Bob Hayes and Mike O'Brien for their care of Chewy.

I would like to thank my wife for all the hours spent helping me write this book. Lauren sacrificed most of her weekends in the last year, along with many weekday nights after working a long day at her job, to help me with this book. Without her input it simply could not have been written. The book is really her story and she equally authored it.

Finally, if Chewy could read human words I would like to thank him for coming into our lives; for sticking with us when we were trying to help him with our fumbling but caring actions. You are the best, Chew boy!